"Fr. Kureethadam has provide
spiritual and theological vision   ...ows how
ordinary Catholics can turn this vision into a personal action plan
for assuming ecological responsibility. A clearly written and
deeply challenging volume."

> —John T. Pawlikowski, OSM
> Professor Emeritus of Social Ethics
> Catholic Theological Union

"This is one of the clearest commentaries that I have read on
Laudato Si'. The author stays faithful to the original text and
manages to distil and even clarify its essential message with
some carefully chosen examples, while not losing nuance. If
anyone is in any doubt that questions to do with ecology are
bound up with issues of poverty and marginalization, they
should read this book. Yet, this author does more than just give
information, this book is inspiring to read, and echoes the same
combination of depth and spirituality that Pope Francis so
wonderfully illustrates himself."

> —Celia Deane-Drummond
> Professor of Theology
> University of Notre Dame

"Fr. Joshtrom Kureethadam has written a powerful and
transformative book. *The Ten Green Commandments* will ignite a
radical environmental effort. He uses elegant words and a
graceful style to open our hearts and rekindle our reverence for
all living systems. His insight, warmth, and care for humanity is
very compelling and supports the important scientific facts that
are the basis for *Laudato Si'*."

> —Jacqueline Miller
> Founder and CEO of Partnerships for Change

The Ten Green Commandments of *Laudato Si'*

Joshtrom Isaac Kureethadam

LITURGICAL PRESS

Collegeville, Minnesota

www.litpress.org

Cover design by Monica Bokinskie. Photo courtesy of Getty Images.

Excerpts from *Laudato Si'* © 2015, Libreria Editrice Vaticana. Used with permission.

Scripture quotations are from New Revised Standard Version Bible © 1989 National Council of the Churches of Christ in the United States of America. Used by permission. All rights reserved worldwide.

Excerpts from the English translation of the *Catechism of the Catholic Church* for use in the United States of America copyright © 1994, United States Catholic Conference, Inc.—Libreria Editrice Vaticana. English translation of the *Catechism of the Catholic Church: Modifications from the Editio Typica* copyright © 1997, United States Catholic Conference, Inc.— Libreria Editrice Vaticana. Used with Permission.

1	2	3	4	5	6	7	8	9

Library of Congress Cataloging-in-Publication Data

Names: Kureethadam, Joshtrom Isaac, author.
Title: The ten green commandments of Laudato si' / Joshtrom Isaac Kureethadam.
Description: Collegeville, Minnesota : Liturgical Press, 2019.
Identifiers: LCCN 2018030692 (print) | LCCN 2018044555 (ebook) | ISBN 9780814663875 (ebook) | ISBN 9780814663639
Subjects: LCSH: Human ecology—Religious aspects—Catholic Church. | Ecotheology. | Catholic Church—Doctrines. | Catholic Church. Pope (2013– : Francis) Laudato si'.
Classification: LCC BX1795.H82 (ebook) | LCC BX1795.H82 K87 2019 (print) | DDC 261.8/8—dc23
LC record available at https://lccn.loc.gov/2018030692

Dedicated to

POPE FRANCIS
for his constant invitation
to care for one another
and for our common home

Contents

Foreword

Professor Myles Allen
Environmental Change Institute
University of Oxford, UK

The publication of *Laudato Si'* marked a very timely, important, and welcome turning point in the global conversation on the future of our climate and environment, and I am delighted to provide a foreword to Joshtrom Isaac Kureethadam's thoughtful, passionate, and deeply personal commentary.

Although some academics have long pointed out that environmental decisions in general, and the climate issue in particular, involved a strong ethical dimension, for all too long they have been seen as a purely pragmatic technical questions. I was particularly struck by how many commentators reacted to the publication of the encyclical with the suggestion that Pope Francis had "no business" to intervene in the climate change debate: for example, a prominent politician remarking, "I don't get economic policy from . . . my pope." If an economic issue involves weighing up the rights of different generations, including those unborn, then where else should we turn for advice?

There is a widely held, and in my view unhealthy, view that climate policy is a purely technical matter to be left to the politicians and their unelected specialist advisors, with perhaps some input from academics—as if ensuring a "safe climate" is somehow analogous to providing "safe drinking water." The analogy is dangerous precisely because it can be used to exclude vitally important voices from the discussion. While Pope Francis has every right to intervene (and has intervened, very effectively, in *Laudato Si'*) to support the right of the poor to safe drinking water, to assess whether a specific water source is safe or not, we turn to the experts, their diagnostic kits and World Health Organization guidelines.

The "safe climate/safe water" mis-analogy has been, perhaps inadvertently, promoted by both sides of the climate debate. On the one hand, the propensity of some academics and environmental activists to focus on "tipping points," "guardrails," and "planetary boundaries" gives a clear impression that there are hard physical limits to the level of climate change that we and the earth as a whole can tolerate. From this, it is a small step to conclude that it is primarily a technical matter, involving more detailed computer models, more careful observations, and (of course!) more research funding to work out what these limits are. Climate policy becomes a matter of keeping within these scientifically determined limits at all costs, and that provided we succeed in doing so, we have nothing to worry about.

On the other hand, the small but vociferous community who take the rather Panglossian position that, in spite of mounting evidence to the contrary, climate change is nothing to worry about are equally keen to talk about "climate catastrophe"—but, in their case, to dismiss it. They know there is little evidence for global catastrophic harm within the planning horizons of today's politicians. Although climate change is taking place in the blink of an eye from the perspective of the Creator, it is overwhelmingly likely that the weather in five to ten years' time will be barely distinguishable from the weather today. People are, in many cases rightly, beginning to notice that the weather they experience now is perceptibly different from the weather they remember as children, but no one could plausibly suggest that these changes amount to a global catastrophe. So, again, it suits the narrative of the Climate Panglossians to argue that dangerous climate change is too remote a possibility for it to be worth doing anything about it.

I myself experienced the unfortunate consequences of this technocratic framing of the climate change issue in the run-up to the ill-fated 2009 Conference of the Parties to the United Nations Framework Convention on Climate Change (UN-FCCC) in Copenhagen. Like many climate scientists, I was repeatedly asked whether I supported statements like "the science dictates" a particular level of emission reduction by 2030. I was unable to do so, not because I didn't personally support early emission reductions, but because it simply wasn't true that they were dictated by climate science. The Copenhagen conference ended in acrimony largely because, I understand, many countries were suspicious they were being corralled into a position on the grounds that it was "dictated by science" when it self-evidently wasn't. Climate policy must be informed by science, but it cannot be dictated by science, which is where *Laudato Si'* is so helpful.

Invoking the picture of "care for our common home," the encyclical makes clear that stewardship of the environment is a matter of curation and cooperation, not simply operating within scientifically determined boundaries. As Pope Francis writes in the introduction, "We need a conversation which includes everyone, since the environmental challenge we are undergoing, and its human roots, concern and affect us all." In his commentary, Kureethadam rightly draws out a common thread in *Laudato Si'* of rejection of technocratic solutions and embrace of a common responsibility. Only as citizens, not consumers, can we "consider goals transcending immediate economic interest."

But how can a conversation that involves over seven billion citizens of this planet ever reach a conclusion? This is where the moral leadership of Pope Francis and other religious leaders plays such an important role. One of the humbling things I have learned over a quarter-century in climate change research (during which, depressingly, the world has warmed by almost half a degree) is that quantifying how the climate system responds to greenhouse gas emissions, to which I have devoted most of my career, is probably the easiest and least important step in deciding what to do about it. This is arguably the only step in the assessment of the climate change issue that does not involve an ethical dimension.

Quantifying the impacts of different levels of warming, and how we value them, are much more challenging and ultimately more important questions, and already ethical issues begin to come into play. An increasingly important issue in the UNFCCC is the question of "Loss and Damage" as countries begin to assess how climate change is impacting them today. These impacts primarily emerge through changing risks of extreme weather events. Some types of events, such as heat waves and episodes of intense rainfall, are becoming more frequent because of climate change. Others, such as intense cold events in winter, are becoming less frequent. Determining how much these frequencies are changing due to external drivers such as rising greenhouse gas concentrations is a matter for meteorologists like myself. But in translating this into an assessment of overall harm, should we include only those harmful events that have occurred and have been made more likely by climate change? Or should we balance this against the harm avoided by hypothetical events that might have occurred, but did not, and were made less likely to occur by climate change? What if these harms affect different people: for example, if those living in the valleys are increasingly vulnerable to floods, while those living in the hills are enjoying lower heating bills in winter?

On an even broader scale, how do we value harm done to the present generation against harm done to the next generation and generations to come? One of the key insights to emerge from physical climate science over the past decade (I wouldn't want to give you the impression we scientists are entirely incidental to this discussion) is the longevity of fossil carbon emissions. Once we release carbon dioxide into the atmosphere, its influence persists indefinitely, continuing to affect the weather and climate for thousands of years. So our emissions today will affect our great-great-grandchildren, unless an intervening generation steps in and pumps that carbon dioxide back out of the atmosphere and "refossilizes" it, a process that would be formidably costly and may not be feasible at all. But how do we weigh our responsibilities to our distant descendants, who will undoubtedly be living in a very different world to our own socially, economically, and environmentally, against our responsibilities to the poor who are alive today?

These are ethical questions and cannot be left to scientists and economists. In *Laudato Si'*, Pope Francis provides us with the necessary moral framework, recognizing the importance of "rejection of every form of self-centeredness and self-absorption" which is at the heart of the Christian message itself. The encyclical has already had a profound impact on the environmental debate in general and the discussion of our response to climate change in particular. In the preparations for the Paris Conference of the UNFCCC in December 2015, there was a much greater emphasis on bottom-up, inclusive initiatives such as the "High Ambition Coalition," resulting in a much more positive and hopeful conclusion, in stark contrast to the acrimony of Copenhagen in 2009.

For the first time, all nations of the world have affirmed their intention to address this global challenge and set themselves what was, to many, a surprisingly ambitious goal. In Article 2, they set out a collective aim "to strengthen the global response to the threat of climate change, in the context of sustainable development and efforts to eradicate poverty, . . . by holding the increase in the global average temperature to well below 2°C above pre-industrial levels, and to pursue efforts to limit the temperature increase to 1.5°C." Going further, in Article 4 they recognized that achieving this goal would require "global peaking of greenhouse gas emissions as soon as possible" and "a balance between anthropogenic emissions by sources and removals by sinks of greenhouse gases in the second half of this century." Stripped of the jargon, this second sentence means an acknowledgment of the need for net zero carbon dioxide emissions before 2100.

Without the support of the leaders of the world's great religions, in which *Laudato Si'* played a central role, it is doubtful the world's governments would have felt able to commit to such an ambitious program. But getting governments to agree in a UN meeting is one thing; bringing on board the world's corporations, great and small, representatives of civil society, and ultimately private citizens will take many years. *Laudato Si'* provides us with the inspiration and moral compass to embark on this journey together. Joshtrom Isaac Kureethadam's book will be a welcome and insightful guide to the reader. But neither is an instruction manual for technocratic planetary management. Perhaps the most important insight in *Laudato Si'*, reaffirmed in Kureethadam's book, is the centrality of a personal response to these challenges and the hope expressed that humanity can, together, "seek a new beginning." I look forward to a continuing conversation between academics and the faithful and hope you will find this book as useful a guide to *Laudato Si'* as I have done.

Preface

"Laudato Si' mi' Signore" ("Praise be to you, my Lord"), the opening line of Saint Francis's *Canticle of Creatures* and the title of Pope Francis's encyclical on care for our common home, best sums up my personal feelings of profound gratitude on completing this volume. I have had the joy and the agony of dealing with ecological concerns for nearly a quarter of a century. Ever since I began to teach cosmology to undergraduates in the early 1990s, I was particularly concerned about the increasingly precarious state of our common planetary home as evidenced by the mounting avalanche of warnings from the scientific community in the last decades. Accordingly, I have tried to pass on to my students all these years not only a sense of awe and wonder before the grandeur and majesty of the infinitely vast universe but also a deep sense of concern for our increasingly fragile common home. Pope Francis's encyclical on care for our common home was therefore deeply reassuring for me. It does respond to the greatest challenge of humanity today even though we have pretended not to see it for too long.

Laudato Si' was itself overdue as a papal encyclical. Nearly ten years ago, I offered a weeklong course on stewardship of creation for a group of committed lay Catholics, as part of the commendable *Living Theology* program run by the British Jesuits. I remember how we dedicated the last session of the course to a sort of brainstorming on what should be the components of a papal encyclical on the important question of creation care. The group felt that such an encyclical was not only necessary but also urgent in the light of what we discussed in the course. This group of lay people had, in fact, anticipated the encyclical. Along with them and scores of others within the church and outside who eagerly, and at times impatiently, awaited a papal encyclical on one of the most defining issues of our times and of Christian living, I praise the Lord for *Laudato Si'*.

I would also like to praise the Lord for Pope Francis, who already in the inaugural Mass of his pontificate stated that the protection of creation, of our common home, and of our common household, especially of the poor and vulnerable, was precisely the service to which the Bishop of Rome is called. I praise the Lord for his immediate predecessors, Pope John Paul II and Pope Benedict, who regularly spoke on ecological issues and in some way prepared the way for *Laudato Si'*. I praise the Lord for religious leaders around the world, the ecumenical patriarch Bartholomew I, in particular, who has been a clear and steady voice in defense of God's creation all these years. I also praise and thank the Lord for the countless array of scientists, scholars, community leaders, environmental movements, grassroots activists, and so many others who have tirelessly dedicated their energies all this while to remind us of the need to care for our imperiled common home before it is too late.

Laudato Si' is the longest of all papal encyclicals. It covers a wide range of issues spanning from climate change to creation theology and from favelas to coral reefs. The sheer number of questions dealt with in the encyclical could make one apprehensive to wade deeper into the text despite its easy language and informal style. The present volume is a modest attempt to gather together in a more accessible package the main ideas of the groundbreaking encyclical of Pope Francis. This is done in terms of the "ten green commandments" for the care of our common home. These green commandments themselves follow the main outline of the six chapters of the encyclical and are arranged according to the scheme of the see-judge-act methodology increasingly used in social sciences.

The present volume offers an exposition of the main themes of the encyclical. It is not an evaluation or a critical appraisal of the text that could be done in more appropriate forums. I have only tried to provide a little guide to understand the encyclical better. I have also attempted to sketch out the wider contexts of Pope Francis's reflections, taking a cue from ecological sciences and environmental discussions. I have cited extensively from the encyclical to let Pope Francis speak directly to the reader.

I need to thank so many people who have made this book possible. I prepared my first commentary on the encyclical within a fortnight of its publication. It was entitled precisely the "ten green commandments of *Laudato Si'* " and served as an introduction to the volume of the proceedings of a conference on sustainability held at the Salesian University in March 2015, which I edited. A number of people who read this introduction encouraged me to take forward my reflections and the present volume is the happy outcome of this journey. I thank Banzelão Julio Teixeira, who read through an earlier draft of the manuscript and offered some useful suggestions. I am deeply indebted to Sr. Helen Carey, FMA, who meticulously proofread the entire manuscript and offered valuable corrections.

I would like to place on record my gratitude to Professor Myles Allen, head of the Climate Change Group of the prestigious Environmental Change Institute at the University of Oxford, for having consented to write a beautiful foreword to the volume. I have found in him, and in many other scientists with whom I have had the opportunity to interact over this period, a profound esteem toward the person of Pope Francis and a real sense of appreciation and gratitude for the moral leadership offered by him on such an important challenge facing humanity today.

For the encouragement and support for the publication of this book, I thank Barry M. Hudock, and the wonderful team at Liturgical Press.

Finally, I ardently pray that this humble volume may contribute to inflame in many hearts the zeal for the care of our common home.

"Send forth your Spirit, O Lord, and renew the face of the earth" (see Ps 104:30).

May 19, 2018
Solemnity of the Pentecost

Introduction

"Francis, Go and Repair My House Which, as You See,
Is Falling into Ruin"

One day in 1205, a young man, son of a wealthy cloth merchant in Assisi, restless and searching for the real goal of his life, walked into the dilapidated church of San Damiano in the outskirts of the town. There occurred something that would radically change the course of his life, the life of the church, and to an extent even of the world. Here is one of the earliest accounts of what happened, from the celebrated biography *Life of Francis* by Bonaventure:

> One day when Francis went out to meditate in the fields he was passing by the church of San Damiano which was threatening to collapse because of extreme age. Inspired by the Spirit, he went inside to pray.
>
> Kneeling before an image of the Crucified, he was filled with great fervour and consolation as he prayed. While his tear-filled eyes were gazing at the Lord's cross, he heard with his bodily ears a voice coming from the cross, telling him three times: "Francis, *go and repair my house which, as you see, is falling into ruin.*"
>
> Trembling with fear, Francis was amazed at the sound of this astonishing voice, since he was alone in the church; and as he received in his heart the power of the divine words, he fell into a state of ecstasy. Returning finally to

1

his senses, he prepared to put his whole heart into obeying
the command he had received. He began zealously to repair the church materially, although the principal intention
of the words referred to that Church which Christ pur-
chased with his own blood, as the Holy Spirit afterward
made him realize. "[1]

God was asking Francis of Assisi to repair the church
which had become dilapidated by the accumulation of excessive wealth, the search for mundane glory, widespread ignorance and immorality among the clergy, and a host of other
problems. Deeply transformed by this mystical experience,
Francis radically changed the course of his life. He began to
spend long hours in prayer in empty caves and country cha-
pels seeking to discern God's will for him. He began to contemplate God's beauty in nature where every flower, every
blade of grass, every little bird, spoke to him of God's infinite
love and glory. He also began to care for the poor and needy
people around him, particularly the lepers who lived as out-
casts in the peripheries of the city. Soon he attracted many
disciples. Together they initiated a gentle yet radical revolution in the church. Their arms were simple but incisive: evan-
gelical poverty, simplicity, humility, and universal love.
Historians today largely concur on how the humble revolution initiated by the *poverello* of Assisi and his followers made
an important contribution in the renewal of the church in the
centuries that followed. Francis was indeed a man raised by
Divine Providence to renew the house of God in those times.

On the evening of March 13, 2013, as the winter sun was
setting over the limpid skies of the eternal city, the large

---

1. Bonaventure, *Leggenda maggiore (Vita di san Francesco d'Assisi), Fonti
francescane* (Padua: Editrici francescane, 2004), 1038.

crowd at St. Peter's square went ecstatic. A plume of white fumes had just begun to spew out of the chimney of the Sistine Chapel accompanied by the continuous pealing of the church bells. They were witnessing a historical moment: the election of a new pope. In no time the sprawling square was filled to capacity as people rushed in from the neighbouring streets and alleys, and television crews began to perch themselves at vantage points. All eyes were fixed on the baroque balcony in the middle of the imposing facade of St. Peter's basilica, draped in red velvet for the occasion, where the new pope was scheduled to appear.

Several minutes later, a shy yet smiling person, clad in white, walked onto the balcony. There was a moment of silence. He was not any of the so-called *papabili* about whom newspaper columns and television channels had extensively gossiped in the days preceding the conclave. The pope-elect, Jorge Mario Bergoglio, the archbishop of Buenos Aires, was better known in the slums of his metropolis than in international media. Then the crowd burst into a thunderous applause and began to chant loudly "Francesco," "Francesco," the endearing name that the new pope had chosen for himself.

Many saw in the election of Pope Francis a divine intervention to "re-build" the Catholic Church in the wake of a stream of scandals and mishaps, factors that some even attributed to the resignation of his predecessor, Pope Benedict. Here was the new Francis who would rebuild the "house" of God that was falling into ruin. Pope Francis did not disappoint. He appeared to have set in motion, in full earnest and with courage, a spate of courageous reforms within the church, reaping some immediate and positive results already.

However, scarcely did anyone realize that the mission of Pope Francis was to rebuild not just the "house" of the church but a much larger one, our very common home.

"Francis, Go and Repair My House Which, as You See, Is Falling into Ruin"

Laudato Si', the encyclical of Pope Francis on creation care, significantly carries the subtitle *On Care for Our Common Home*.[2] It is not about mere "environment" that the encyclical is concerned with, but about the fate of our very home. In fact, the opening chapter carries the title "What is happening to our common home."

Today, our common planetary home is falling into ruin. We are on the brink of an unprecedented global challenge regarding the sustainability of our common home, which places a question mark on the very future of human civilization. The horror movie of the destruction of our home planet, the only abode for complex forms of life in the entire universe—at least as far as we know—may now begin to play out before our very eyes. We are running out of time, we are in the eleventh hour. It appears that we are condemned to a warming world, sweltering temperatures, melting glaciers, and inundated shorelines in the decades and centuries to come. We may be condemning future generations to a common home in ruins.

We are indeed playing a reckless gamble with our common home and ultimately with our own destiny and survival. Our actions today will determine the future not only of the present generations but also of future generations for millennia. As Seán McDonagh points out, "If this generation does not act, no future generation will be able to undo the damage that this generation has caused to the planet."[3] We are indeed living in a critical and crucial moment regarding the habitability of our very common home and of the future of humanity.

2. Pope Francis, Encyclical Letter *Laudato Si'* (Vatican City: Libreria Editrice Vaticana, 2015).

3. Seán McDonagh, *The Death of Life: The Horror of Extinction* (Dublin: Columba Press, 2004), 151.

It is against this background that Pope Francis appears to have stepped into the scene. He too appears to have given a receptive hearing to the command of the Lord, like his namesake centuries ago, to "go and repair my house." In the encyclical *Laudato Si'*, Pope Francis urges the Catholic Church, the Christian communities around the world, followers of other religious tradition, and all people of good will to earnestly begin to care for our common home that is beginning to crumble.

Francis is the first pope to dedicate an entire encyclical—one of the highest forms of papal magisterium and next only to the Apostolic Constitution—to the question of the care of our common home. Pope Francis, given his towering moral stature and his unique qualities as a much loved and charismatic leader around the world—"an authority in authority"[4] as it is widely acknowledged—is uniquely poised to offer leadership in efforts to address and respond to the crisis of our common home. However, he is not alone and can count on a large cloud of witnesses in this regard. As the pope himself acknowledges in the encyclical, "the reflections of numerous scientists, philosophers, theologians and civic groups" have "enriched the Church's thinking on these questions" (7).[5]

In the preamble to the encyclical, the pope mentions some outstanding witnesses within the Christian communities with regard to the stewardship of our common home. He begins with his own predecessors in the first place. Pope Francis opens his survey of the magisterium of his predecessors with Pope Paul VI who had "referred to the ecological concern as 'a tragic

---

4. Daniel R. DiLeo, "*Laudato Si'*, Interest, and Engagement: An Account via Catholic Public Theology and Authority," *Environment: Science and Policy for Sustainable Development* 57/6 (2015), 7.

5. The numbers in parentheses following quotations of *Laudato Si'* refer to paragraph numbers in the encyclical.

consequence' of unchecked human activity" (4). Paul VI had admonished way back in 1971: "Due to an ill-considered exploitation of nature, humanity runs the risk of destroying it and becoming in turn a victim of this degradation"[6] (4).

Pope John Paul II was particularly sensitive on ecological issues and had proclaimed St. Francis of Assisi as the model of ecologists already in 1979.[7] John Paul II has left a rich heritage of teachings regarding humanity's relationship with the natural world.[8] Pope Francis makes a succinct summary of it in *Laudato Si'*, part of which we will cite here.

> Saint John Paul II became increasingly concerned about this issue. In his first encyclical he warned that human beings frequently seem "to see no other meaning in their natural environment than what serves for immediate use and consumption."[9] Subsequently, he would call for a global ecological *conversion*.[10] At the same time, he noted that little effort had been made to "safeguard the moral conditions for an authentic *human ecology*."[11] The destruction of the human environment is extremely serious, not only because God has entrusted the world to us men and women, but because human life is itself a gift which must be defended from various forms of debasement. Every effort to protect and

6. Pope Paul VI, Apostolic Letter *Octogesima Adveniens* (1971), 21: *AAS* 63 (1971), 416–17.

7. Pope John Paul II, Apostolic Letter *Inter Sanctos* (1979): *AAS* 71 (1979), 1509–10.

8. See Marybeth Lorbiecki, *Following St. Francis: John Paul II's Call for Ecological Conversion* (New York: Rizzoli Ex Libris, 2014).

9. John Paul II, Encyclical Letter *Redemptor Hominis* (1979), 15: *AAS* 71 (1979), 287.

10. Cf. John Paul II, *Catechesis* (17 January 2001), 4: *Insegnamenti* 41/1 (2001), 179.

11. John Paul II, Encyclical Letter *Centesimus Annus* (1991), 38: *AAS* 83 (1991), 841.

improve our world entails profound changes in "lifestyles, models of production and consumption, and the established structures of power which today govern societies."[12] (5)

We may also recall John Paul II's important Message for the World Day of Peace in 1990, "Peace with God the Creator, Peace with All of Creation," the first papal document to be entirely devoted to ecological questions. In this concise but incisive document, the pope had described the ecological crisis as a moral problem and called for a radical change of our lifestyles to overcome the crisis.

Pope Benedict had been a steady voice in the defence of creation during his pontificate, meriting him the appellative of a "green pope."[13] He did not stop at symbolic gestures like installing solar panels on the roof of the Paul VI Hall, the main auditorium of the Vatican, but on diverse occasions intervened for the defence of the natural world. Pope Francis evidences the integral approach of Pope Benedict on ecological questions when he cites: "He [Pope Benedict] observed that the world cannot be analyzed by isolating only one of its aspects, since 'the book of nature is one and indivisible,' and includes the environment, life, sexuality, the family, social relations, and so forth" (6). According to Pope Benedict, "The misuse of creation begins when we no longer recognize any higher instance than ourselves, when we see nothing else but ourselves"[14] (6). Rowan Williams, the former Anglican archbishop of Canterbury, is of the opinion that *Laudato Si'* is in some way a natural development of the Christian humanism

12. Ibid., 58: *AAS*, 863.

13. See Woodeene Koenig-Bricker, *Ten Commandments for the Environment: Pope Benedict XVI Speaks Out for Creation and Justice* (Notre Dame, IN: Ave Maria Press, 2009), 1–10.

14. Pope Benedict XVI, *Address to the Clergy of the Diocese of Bolzano-Bressanone* (6 August 2008): *AAS* 100 (2008), 634.

of Pope Benedict's theology, especially as found in *Caritas in Veritate*.[15]

In the preamble to *Laudato Si'*, Pope Francis takes pains to evidence the significant contribution also of the ecumenical patriarch Bartholomew I, known as the "green patriarch" for his commitment to ecological questions for nearly a quarter of a century.[16] The leadership of the ecumenical patriarch on ecological issues is not only acknowledged by Pope Francis but also drawn upon and cited approvingly. The pope dedicates two extensive paragraphs to present some of the key ecological intuitions of Bartholomew like the concept of ecological sin, the need for repentance, the spiritual and theological roots of the problem, and the vital importance of asceticism in responding to the crisis. The pope retains as highly important the patriarch's teachings on the concept of ecological sin, namely that abuse of creation on the part of humanity is truly a sin against humanity and against the very Creator. For "to commit a crime against the natural world is a sin against ourselves and a sin against God"[17] (8).

Apart from the magisterium of his own immediate predecessors and of the "green patriarch" Bartholomew I, there is yet another significant source from which Pope Francis has drawn extensively. It is the rich and varied corpus of the statements of Catholic Bishops' Conferences around the world in the last few decades on the problem of the current

15. Rowan Williams, "Embracing Our Limits: The Lessons of *Laudato Si'*," *Commonweal* (9 October 2015), 13.

16. For a discussion of the ecumenical context of the encyclical, see the contribution of John Chryssavgis, theological advisor to the ecumenical patriarch on environmental issues: "Pope Francis' *Laudato Si'*: A Personal Response, An Ecumenical Reflection," *Phromena* 31 (2016), 17–21.

17. *Address in Santa Barbara, California* (8 November 1997); cf. John Chryssavgis, *On Earth as in Heaven: Ecological Vision and Initiatives of Ecumenical Patriarch Bartholomew* (New York: Fordham University Press, 2012).

ecological degradation and on the importance of creation care. Since the 1980s, many Bishops' Conferences have issued statements on the deteriorating state of our common planetary home and on specific ecological hazards in their respective regions. In his encyclical on creation care, Pope Francis allows the papal magisterium to be fed from the teachings of his brother bishops around the world—the so-called "regional magisterium."[18] It is totally unprecedented and reflects the pope's desire to build a more collegial and participatory church. *Laudato Si'* carries citations from several national and regional bishops' conferences, as many as twenty-one of them, spread across five continents.

Pope Francis's encyclical thus draws from a huge repertoire of sources on ecological reflection within the Catholic and Christian communities, in other religions, and in the wide spectrum of empirical, human, and social sciences. It is a fitting approach for an encyclical eager to dialogue with all people of good will on the destiny of our planetary home.

The rich and varied sources of *Laudato Si'* make it a very comprehensive and wide-ranging text, surveying a sweeping range of issues, spanning from climate change to creation theology and from favelas to coral reefs. It is the longest of all encyclicals so far and covers a wide range of ecological, social, political, economic, theological, anthropological, cultural, and related questions. Indeed, the encyclical offers so much that it makes its reading and application not very easy. The scope of the present volume is to gather together in a more accessible package the main messages of the groundbreaking encyclical of Pope Francis on care for our common home. We shall do so by presenting the "ten green commandments" of the encyclical.

---

18. Clemens Sedmark, "Traditional Concerns, New Language? Reflections on *Laudato Si'*," *The Heythrop Journal* 58 (2017), 942.

The main messages of the encyclical can be summed up in terms of "ten green commandments" from Pope Francis. Here they are:

I. Earth, our common home, is in peril. Take care of it.

II. Listen to the cry of the poor who are the disproportionate victims of the crisis of our common home.

III. Rediscover a theological vision of the natural world as good news (gospel).

IV. Recognize that the abuse of creation is ecological sin.

V. Acknowledge the deeper human roots of the crisis of our common home.

VI. Develop an integral ecology as we are all interrelated and interdependent.

VII. Learn a new way of dwelling in our common home and manage it more responsibly through a new economics and a new political culture.

VIII. Educate toward ecological citizenship through change of lifestyles.

IX. Embrace an ecological spirituality that leads to communion with all of God's creatures.

X. Care for our common home by cultivating the ecological virtues of praise, gratitude, care, justice, work, sobriety, and humility.

The ten green commandments of *Laudato Si'* can themselves be best understood in terms of the see-judge-act methodology, popular in the church since the Second Vatican Council. We shall offer below a rapid summary of the ten green commandments enumerated above within the see-judge-act framework. It could be a sort of "three-dimensional" view of the encyclical which could help us to understand the text in greater depth.

The first two green commandments of *Laudato Si'* are concerned about "seeing" the precarious situation of our common home. This is precisely the scope of the opening chapter of the encyclical entitled "What is happening to our common home." Here Pope Francis speaks of two cries: the cry of the earth and the cry of the poor. The pope begins with a physical description of the crisis of our common home. The encyclical employs the best of scientific evidence—a fact acknowledged by many prominent members of the scientific community in their initial reactions to the encyclical—to look at the current state of our world. It goes on to offer an empirical description of the challenges facing our common home: pollution and climate change, loss of biodiversity, depletion of natural resources including water, decline in the quality of human life, and the breakdown of society. The second green commandment speaks of the cry of the poor. The ecological crisis is not just a physical problem but also a deeply moral crisis. It is so precisely because of the disproportionate impacts of the crisis on poor people and communities around the world. Ecological questions need to be considered therefore within the ethical framework of eco-justice.

The next three green commandments are concerned about "judging" the precarious situation of our common home. The third green commandment offers the theological criterion to judge the crisis of our common home. Pope Francis invites us to see the world from a religious perspective, recognizing in the natural world the "gospel of creation"—the title of the second chapter of the encyclical. For believers, as Pope Francis points out, the world is not just nature but creation. Our world is indeed "good news" which reveals the love, beauty, and glory of the Creator. As is evident in the fourth green commandment, Pope Francis describes the destruction of our common home as sin, drawing also from the rich magisterium of Ecumenical Patriarch Bartholomew in this regard. Ecological sin is the rupture of relationships with the natural world, our fellow human beings, and the Creator and calls for repentance on the part of humanity. Repentance begins by acknowledging our human responsibility in defiling our common home, as claimed by the fifth green commandment. In fact, the third chapter of the encyclical is entitled "The Human Roots of the Ecological Crisis." The deepest roots of the crisis can be found in modern anthropocentrism based on which human beings place themselves at the center of the universe, usurping the primacy of the Creator and ruthlessly pillaging the rest of creation.

The last five green commandments are concerned with "acting," after having seen and judged the profound crisis of our common home. The pope dedicates the last three chapters of the encyclical to discuss ways and means to respond to the crisis. As evidenced by the sixth green commandment, the pope argues that we stand in need of an integral approach to understand, evaluate, and respond to the crisis of our common home. Pope Francis dedicates an entire chapter to the concept of integral ecology. The seventh green commandment highlights the emphasis placed by Pope Francis in the encyclical on a new way of dwelling in our common home and managing it more responsibly. This is done in the fifth chapter of the encyclical entitled "Lines of Action." The pope speaks of the importance of acting together at the international, national, and local levels to safeguard our common home. The pope also calls for a new economy and a new political order both of which need to be at the service of the common good. In the last chapter of the encyclical, Pope Francis speaks of the two basic areas of ecological education and ecological spirituality, so vital for the care of our common home. Pope Francis calls for ecological education capable of establishing a new covenant between humanity and the natural world. He also speaks of the variety of settings for education to ecological citizenship: schools, families, media, catechesis, and houses of religious formation. The pope also traces the contours of an ecological spirituality for our times. Such a spirituality is deeply incarnational and offers a sacramental vision of the natural world as permeated by divine presence. As the pope points out, the whole of creation bears the trinitarian imprint as it is ultimately God's handiwork, created and constantly sustained by God's infinite love.

The last of the green commandments of *Laudato Si'* concerns the ecological virtues that we need to cultivate in order to become creative and responsible stewards of our common home. The ecological virtues do not receive special treatment in the encyclical as such, but are mentioned repeatedly throughout the text. They are signposts that indicate the road we need to travel in caring for our common planetary home. We shall highlight seven of the ecological virtues in our commentary of *Laudato Si'*: praise, gratitude, care, justice, work, sobriety, and humility.

Through a detailed presentation of each of the ten green commandments mentioned above, we now embark on the journey of study and meditation of *Laudato Si'*, Pope Francis's encyclical letter on care for our common home.

PART ONE: **SEEING**
(Understanding the Crisis of Our Common Home)

GREEN COMMANDMENT I
Take Care of Our Common Home in Peril

GREEN COMMANDMENT II
Listen to the Cry of the Poor

Our first two green commandments are about seeing and understanding the current degradation of our common home. In the very first chapter of the encyclical entitled "What is happening to our common home," Pope Francis offers a rather holistic understanding of the contemporary ecological crisis and invites us to "hear both the cry of the earth and the cry of the poor" (49). According to him, the ecological crisis is indeed "one complex crisis which is both social and environmental" (139).

The first green commandment offers a physical understanding of the crisis of our common home with the support of credible scientific evidence. We begin with a reflection on the very expression "common home," which clearly signals Pope Francis's desire to move beyond the "environmental" straightjacket in which ecological questions have been mostly addressed in the past. We then go on to discuss the main physical manifestations of the ecological crisis highlighted in the encyclical. These include pollution and waste, climate change and its impacts, the depletion of natural resources, the scarcity of fresh drinking water, and the problem of species extinction and biodiversity loss. The crisis facing our common home is truly global and totally unprecedented.

The second green commandment tells us that the contemporary ecological crisis is not just a physical problem but is also a deeply moral crisis. It is so since the poor are the early and disproportionate victims of the crisis of our common home. The encyclical links the cry of the earth inextricably with the cry of the poor. Pope Francis pays special attention in the encyclical to the ecological hazards faced by poor communities, indigenous groups, and future generations. The ecological crisis raises the question of eco-justice and deals with thorny issues like the ecological debt that the developed world and richer communities owes to the poorer nations and communities around the world.

GREEN COMMANDMENT I

Take Care of Our Common Home in Peril

The first of the green commandments of *Laudato Si'* tells us that Earth is our common home and that we need to care for it. The precarious state of the earth is the fundamental reason for the pope to devote, for the first time in the history of Catholic social teachings, an entire encyclical to care for our common home. This is evident in the very subtitle of the text. It is about "our common home" that he "would like to enter into dialogue with all people" (3). The expression *our common home* occurs several times in the encyclical, and the need to care for it is the *leitmotiv* of the entire document.

We shall reflect below on the paradigm shift ushered in by Pope Francis in the use of the expression *common home*, moving away from the talk about the "environment" that has dominated the ecological discourse in the last few decades. We will also dwell on the uniqueness of planet Earth as a unique "home" for life in the infinitely vast universe. We will then go on to examine the main physical manifestations of the crisis of our common home as outlined in the encyclical: pollution and waste, climate change and its impacts, the depletion of natural resources and especially the scarcity of fresh drinking water, and the unprecedented scales of biodiversity loss. The pope warns that we risk the danger of leaving an uninhabitable planetary home for future generations if we are not willing to change radically the course of our current civilization.

"Our Common Home": A Paradigm Shift

In talking about Earth as our common home, Pope Francis ushers in a major paradigm shift. The crisis that humanity faces today is the crisis of our very common home. The contemporary ecological crisis is not merely an "environmental" problem or even a host of environmental problems, as it is generally supposed. It is about the crisis of our very common home.

For too long, the ecological crisis has been relegated to a set of environmental problems.[1] We have remained complacent, seeing more space allocated to environmental issues in newspaper columns, on television channels, on bookshop shelves, and increasingly even in school and university curricula. As a result, for most people, *environment* has meant merely something external and outside of themselves, and as such has remained a peripheral and secondary concern. We have become complacent with the belief that a bit of recycling and use of fluorescent electric bulbs and similar tricks are all that it takes to be *environment-friendly*. We have been content to leave environmental questions to the Greens and die-hard environmental activists at the local level and to yearly high-level summits under the auspices of the United Nations on the global arena. In the meantime, we have carried on with our routine lives, consuming material goods with increasingly rapacious appetites, enthralled by the glittering

1. Joshtrom Isaac Kureethadam, *Creation in Crisis: Science, Ethics, Theology* (New York: Orbis, 2014), 1–2.

promises of the advertisement industry, and lulled by the beliefs subtly driven home by the corporate industry and mainstream media that environmental concerns are, after all, only peripheral and marginal.

In *Laudato Si'*, Pope Francis reminds us of what we are really sleepwalking into: a possible collapse of our very home, with dire implications for the members of our common household. The encyclical proposes a sort of a paradigm shift in understanding and dealing with the crisis facing our home planet. In fact, if we were to follow the etymological route, the crisis has to do with the discourse (*logos*) centered around our very common home (*oikos*). It is an *eco-logic*al crisis, having to do with the fate of our very home. Earth is our home more than the mere environment that happens to surround us. Earth is the home that engendered us and sustains us. Earth is not merely an environment that we can swap for another one, by migrating somewhere else when our home planet is degraded beyond redemption, like it is sometimes presented in popular science fiction and in the techno-savvy media. Earth is our home, and our only home. We are Earthlings, *imago mundi*, formed from the dust of the earth, inhabitants of the common home of Earth.

Breaking free of the environmental jargon in referring to the ecological crisis as the possible collapse of our common home adds a deeply existential dimension to the whole discussion. Seen in this way, we are not speaking of questions external and marginal to us. We are not talking about one of the many challenges that humanity has to face—and we know that there is no dearth of them. Instead, we are grappling with the destiny of our common home, indeed, humanity's common destiny, along with that of the rest of the biotic community. Without our common home, we cannot live and live well. When we pollute and despoil our common home, we are endangering the quality of our own life, our own well-being, and that of other living beings on Earth, as well as of future generations, our children, and their children. Evidently, one cannot remain indifferent to, but must be passionate about, the crisis of our common home and of our common household.

In a very insightful way, Pope Benedict XVI had summed up this important truth in the *Message for the World Day of Peace* in 2008 when he said that "for the human family, this home is the Earth" and that it is "essential to *sense* that the Earth is *our common home*."[2]

In *Laudato Si'*, Pope Francis tells us that it is fundamental to recover the perception of our Earth as our common home. Life, human life, civilization, religion, philosophy, art, music, literature, science and technology, and a thousand other artifacts of human culture have been possible because there is the common home of the Earth to dwell in, and not vice versa! In fact, what is primary in this sense is being in this home, and the rest, however important, is only secondary, because without the former the latter does not, and cannot, exist. Without our common home, we cannot exist and flourish. Earth can exist without modern humans, as it has done for over 99.9 percent of its history. But we cannot exist without our common home.

The time has come to call the ecological crisis for what it really is—a possible collapse of our very home, with dire implications for the members of our common household. This is what Pope Francis does in *Laudato Si': On Care for Our Common Home*. The pope speaks of our common home in very intimate and "homely" terms as a *sister* and as a *mother* in the very first paragraph of the encyclical. Referring to his name-

2. Pope Benedict XVI, *The Human Family, A Community of Peace* (Message for the World Day of Peace, 1 January 2008), nn. 7–8. The italics are mine.

sake, the pope writes: "Saint Francis of Assisi reminds us that our common home is like a sister with whom we share our life and a beautiful mother who opens her arms to embrace us" (1). According to the pope, "We need only take a frank look at the facts to see that our common home is falling into serious disrepair" (61). The pope points out that we have inflicted great harm on our common home "by our irresponsible use and abuse of the goods with which God has endowed her," and "she 'groans in travail' (*Rom* 8:22)" (2). As he says in the introduction to the encyclical, the protection of our common home is an "urgent challenge" (13).

The paradigm shift of *Laudato Si'* consists in Pope Francis's reminder to humanity that our common home is really in peril and that we need to begin to care for it before it is too late.

Earth, A Unique Home for Life

The understanding of Earth as our common home proposed in *Laudato Si'* is, in fact, as ancient as the book of Genesis, the very first verses of which take us to the dawn of creation.[3] The creation narrative, unfolding as a majestic cosmic drama that spans over six celestial days, is centered around the preparation of a "home" for all living beings, including humans. Within the vault of the heavens, a formless earth is lovingly fashioned by the Creator into a beautiful home, separating the dry land from the waters, adorning it with trees and vegetation, flowers and fruits, and hosting there living things of every kind, including birds, fishes, and animals. In fact, animals, and human beings themselves, are created only on the very last day, only after a proper abode has been prepared for them—a home to dwell in! The

3. Kureethadam, *Creation in Crisis*, 4.

sequence of events in the creation saga is not casual. It is only after a home has been prepared that life, including human life, can be hosted there. Earth is this home for humanity and for the rest of the commonwealth of life.

Significantly, most recent advances in astronomy and life sciences have shed light on the magnificent process in which Earth became the home for life that we are familiar with today.[4] The building blocks necessary for the construction of our common home were originally created and gradually molded in the cosmic furnace of the universe over billions of years. Privileged to cruise through space in the right niche, at the right distance from its home star, our home planet, which was initially only a cauldron of gaseous material and dust of heavy elements, gradually evolved to become the home for life.

Earth became a home for life through a concomitance of myriad factors.[5] There is, first of all, its position in the solar system, ninety-three million miles distant from the sun, a distance suitable for maintaining an optimal temperature that allows water to remain liquid, a fundamental requirement for life to exist and flourish. Its present position also guarantees the right gravitational pull from the sun, from its own moon— which keeps the earth spinning at the right speed and tilting at the right angle, factors that affect the present day-night cycle and the tides in the oceans—and even from a fellow planet like Jupiter which curiously influences the stability of Earth's orbit. The twenty-three-and-a-half-degree inclination of the earth to the sun creates the seasons and makes agriculture possible. The earth also has the right mass to possess the proper gravitational attraction that in turn entitles it to have its own atmosphere, unlike the moon which does not have

---

4. See ibid., 16–21.
5. Ibid. 22–23.

one and where consequently life can never evolve as it did on Earth. Earth retains an atmosphere and water at its surface because of the protective magnetic field generated in its liquid iron/nickel core. The magnetic field also acts as a protective shield from dangerous ionizing radiations from the solar wind, while the ozone layer in the upper layers of the atmosphere blocks out the harmful ultraviolet rays. The atmosphere on Earth has the right composition of gases conducive to life: nitrogen, oxygen, carbon dioxide, and others. Our home planet also enjoys the right greenhouse effect which warms up the atmosphere to the optimum temperature.

The Earth is indeed the "garden planet" of the universe,[6] where life had a magnificent evolution from single cells to the extravagant complexity of today. We remain awestruck by the wonderful saga of how our single planet became a marvellous "home," where life evolved from single cells to conscious beings like us through complex processes that unfolded over millions and millions of years. Earth is what a 2011 document from the Pontifical Academy of Sciences called "a planet blessed with the gift of life"![7] The group of eminent scientists who were also among the principal scientific advisors of Pope Francis in the drafting of the encyclical wrote:

> *We all live in the same home.* By acting now, in the spirit of common but differentiated responsibility, we accept our duty to one another and to *the stewardship of a planet blessed with the gift of life.* We are committed to ensuring that all inhabitants of this planet receive their daily bread, fresh air to breathe and clean water to drink as we are aware

6. See *The Cry of the Earth: A Pastoral Reflection on Climate Change by the Irish Catholic Bishops' Conference* (2009), 7.

7. Pontificia Academia Scientiarum, *Fate of Mountain Glaciers in the Anthropocene: A Report by the Working Group Commissioned by the Pontifical Academy of Sciences* (5 May 2011), 2, 15.

that, if we want justice and peace, *we must protect the habitat that sustains us.*[8]

Laudato Si' is concerned about the precarious state of Earth, our unique common planetary home blessed with the gift of life.

Our Common Home Is in Peril

Laudato Si' begins with taking stock of what is happening to our common home, consonant with the see-judge-act methodology employed throughout the encyclical by Pope Francis. The very first chapter of the encyclical is entitled "What is happening to our common home." The starting point of the encyclical is thus the precarious state of our common home, a totally "unprecedented" (17) situation in which we find ourselves. The pope begins with a physical description of the crisis of our common home, basing himself on solid scientific evidence and carefully selected empirical data, as he himself states: "drawing on the results of the best scientific research available today" (15). He enumerates the main challenges facing our common home, all of which have a detrimental impact on the quality of human life and the stability of human communities around the world. He invites humanity to face "those questions which are troubling us today and which we can no longer sweep under the carpet" (19).

As Pope Francis indicates, the problem is precisely with the "rapidification" of changes that human activities are causing to the sustainability of our home planet. "Although change is part of the working of complex systems, the speed with which human activity has developed contrasts with the

8. Ibid. The italics are mine.

naturally slow pace of biological evolution" (18). Here it may be recalled, by way of example, how the current rates of extinction of species exceed those of the historical past by several orders of magnitude. According to scientists, the normal background rates of extinction is roughly 0.1–1.0 extinctions per million species per year.[9] But, as per the *Millennium Ecosystem Assessment*, "Over the past few hundred years, humans have increased species extinction rates by as much as 1,000 times the background rates that were typical over Earth's history."[10] In fact, scientists fear that extinction rates will increase to the order of 1,000 to 10,000 times background rates over the coming decades.[11] The rapidity with which human activities are altering ecosystems is alarming indeed. In a similar way, the emissions of greenhouse gases from human activities causing climate change is at least a hundred times faster than the natural rates.[12]

In *Laudato Si'*, Pope Francis offers a masterly synthesis of the manifold manifestations of the contemporary ecological crisis, the crisis of our very home: pollution and waste, climate change, depletion of natural resources especially water, and biodiversity loss. These "several aspects of the present ecological crisis" (15) are what Pope Francis calls "cracks in the planet that we inhabit" (163).

Significantly, the pope begins the description of the defilement of our common home with pollution and waste. In fact, our awareness of the precarious state of our home planet

9. Millennium Ecosystem Assessment, *Ecosystems and Human Wellbeing: Biodiversity Synthesis* (Washington: World Resources Institute, 2005), 21.

10. Ibid., 3.

11. Ibid., 43. See also Henrique M. Pereira et al., "Scenarios for Global Biodiversity in the 21st Century," *Science* 330 (2010), 1497.

12. Pontificia Academia Scientiarum, *Fate of Mountain Glaciers in the Anthropocene*, 4.

began more than fifty years ago, precisely with the problem
of pollution. It was highlighted by the classical work of Rachel Carson in 1962: *The Silent Spring*,[13] which called attention
to the health impacts of pollution. Pollution is a distinctly
modern phenomenon which began with the onset of the
Industrial Revolution and has peaked in the last few decades
of economic expansion. In fact, the economic growth and
industrial development of the modern era has a heavy bill
attached to it, namely, the pollution of our planetary home.
Human activities, modern industrial and agricultural activities in particular, appear to have polluted almost all areas of
our common home: the air, the land, and the waters. The
pope offers a long list of the types of pollution "caused by
transport, industrial fumes, substances which contribute to
the acidification of soil and water, fertilizers, insecticides,
fungicides, herbicides and agrotoxins in general" (20). The
encyclical even speaks of "mental pollution" on account of
the overload of information in our age of internet communication, which often "has more to do with devices and dis-
plays than with other people and with nature" (47).

Pope Francis is particularly critical of the problem of waste,
a detrimental residue of our modern consumer culture. "Each
year hundreds of millions of tons of waste are generated,
much of it non-biodegradable, highly toxic and radioactive,
from homes and businesses, from construction and demolition
sites, from clinical, electronic and industrial sources" (21). He
also notes "that approximately a third of all food produced is
discarded" and denounces that "whenever food is thrown out
it is as if it were stolen from the table of the poor"[14] (50). He
points to the real and deeper source of the problem of waste:
"a throwaway culture" which "quickly reduces things to rub-

13. Rachel Carson, *Silent Spring* (Boston: Houghton Mifflin, 1962).
14. Pope Francis, *Catechesis* (5 June 2013): *Insegnamenti* 1/1 (2013),
280.

bish" (22). Pope Francis masterly sums up the harm that human pollution and mindless waste are causing to our beautiful home. "The earth, our home, is beginning to look more and more like an immense pile of filth!" (21).

The encyclical then takes up the most important of the challenges to our common home today, namely, climate change. Pope Francis sees "climate as a common good, belonging to all and meant for all." He speaks forthrightly of the scientific consensus on the issue of climate change: "A very solid scientific consensus indicates that we are presently witnessing a disturbing warming of the climate system." He also backs the scientific convergence that "most global warming in recent decades is due to the great concentration of greenhouse gases (carbon dioxide, methane, nitrogen oxides and others) released mainly as a result of human activity" (23). The pope also points to some of the main sources of climate change. "The problem is aggravated by a model of development based on the intensive use of fossil fuels, which is at the heart of the worldwide energy system. Another determining factor has been an increase in changed uses of the soil, principally deforestation for agricultural purposes" (23).

In the encyclical, the pope also refers to several of the more conspicuous impacts of climate change like "an increase of extreme weather events," "a constant rise in the sea level" (23), pressure on the "availability of essential resources like drinking water, energy and agricultural production in warmer regions," "the extinction of part of the planet's biodiversity," "the melting in the polar ice caps and in high altitude plains," "the loss of tropical forests," "the acidification of the oceans" with consequences for the marine food chain. The pope warns that "if present trends continue, this century may well witness extraordinary climate change and an unprecedented destruction of ecosystems, with serious consequences for all of us." He notes, for example, how "a rise in the sea level, for example, can create extremely serious situations, if we consider that a quarter of the world's population lives on the coast or nearby, and that the majority of our megacities are situated in coastal areas" (24).

Carrying on with the description of the alarming situation of our common home currently, the encyclical moves on to the question of the fast depletion of natural resources. We are not only despoiling our common home but also wasting away and fast draining up the finite resources of our common household. The pope does not mask his staunch critique of current levels of consumption by the rich that have led to the exploitation of our home planet beyond acceptable limits: "We all know that it is not possible to sustain the present level of consumption in developed countries and wealthier sectors of society, where the habit of wasting and discarding has reached unprecedented levels" (27).

The encyclical takes up in particular the question of fresh water, the very source of life and the most critical of all natural resources. "Fresh drinking water is an issue of primary importance, since it is indispensable for human life and for supporting terrestrial and aquatic ecosystems. Sources of fresh water are necessary for health care, agriculture and industry" (28). The pope is particularly concerned about "the quality of water available to the poor" which leads to water-related diseases and even deaths (29). In *Laudato Si'*, Pope Francis affirms the universal right to accessible drinking water and is critical toward the "growing tendency, despite its scarcity, to privatize this resource, turning it into a commodity subject to the laws of the market" (30). Aware that "acute water shortage may occur within a few decades unless urgent action is taken" (31), the encyclical also points to the danger that scarcity of water or its control by large multinational businesses may become a major source of conflict in this century.[15] We

15. Cf. Francis, *Greeting to the Staff of FAO* (20 November 2014): *AAS* 106 (2014), 985.

may conclude with the pope's affirmation that *"access to safe drinking water is a basic and universal human right, since it is essential to human survival and, as such, is a condition for the exercise of other human rights"* (30).

The last of the physical manifestations of the crisis of our common home is the current loss of biodiversity to which the encyclical dedicates relatively ample space. It may be recalled here how there exists a unanimous consensus in the scientific community today that the Earth is on the verge of a sixth mass extinction of species and consequent loss of biodiversity. The pope too begins by taking stock of the gravity of the biodiversity crisis. "Each year sees the disappearance of thousands of plant and animal species which we will never know, which our children will never see, because they have been lost for ever" (33).

While the species are extremely important resources for meeting human needs like nutrition and medicine and for regulating ecosystems, the encyclical invites us not to overlook "the fact that they have value in themselves" (33). In fact, the proper functioning of the planet's ecosystems and of our common planetary home as a whole requires all species, including "fungi, algae, worms, insects, reptiles and an innumerable variety of microorganisms." The pope notes how "some less numerous species, although generally unseen, nonetheless play a critical role in maintaining the equilibrium of a particular place" (34). While discussing biodiversity, the encyclical also refers to the oceans which "not only contain the bulk of our planet's water supply, but also most of the immense variety of living creatures, many of them still unknown to us and threatened for various reasons." According to the pope, "Particularly threatened are marine organisms which we tend to overlook, like some forms of plankton; they represent a significant element in the ocean food chain, and species used for our food ultimately depend on them" (40). The pope is especially sensitive to the alarming state of the world's coral reefs and uses an appropriate quote from the pastoral letter of the bishops of the Philippines:

> In tropical and subtropical seas, we find coral reefs comparable to the great forests on dry land, for they shelter approximately a million species, including fish, crabs, molluscs, sponges and algae. Many of the world's coral reefs are already barren or in a state of constant decline. "Who turned the wonderworld of the seas into underwater cemeteries bereft of colour and life?"[16] (41)

In presenting the multiple physical manifestations of the contemporary ecological crisis, *Laudato Si'* succeeds in driving home a strong message about the magnitude of the precarious situation of our common home. The crisis of our common home is not just climate change or any other singular phenomenon. Our common home is pulled down by several interlinked physical crises.

The Specter of Leaving an Uninhabitable Home to Future Generations

Today the capacity of the earth to be truly a home for all of humanity and for all living beings is increasingly placed in jeopardy. As Pope Francis points out, "Never have we so hurt and mistreated our common home as we have in the last two hundred years" (53). We are destroying our own common home! We are also playing a huge and mindless gamble with the future of our common planetary home and of our fellow

---

16. Catholic Bishops' Conference of the Philippines, Pastoral Letter *What is Happening to our Beautiful Land?* (29 January 1988).

human beings—especially the future generations—and of our fellow species, members of our common household. The closing lines of the London Geological Society's 2010 statement on climate change would be appropriate to remember here: "Many climate change processes have long time lags, so future generations will have to deal with the consequences. Recovery of the earth's climate in the absence of any mitigation measures could take 100,000 years or more, which is indeed a dreadful possibility."[17] On a similar note, it may be remembered that the fate of biological diversity on Earth for the next ten million years will almost certainly be determined during the next fifty to one hundred years by the activities of a single species—the *Homo sapiens* which has unwittingly achieved the ability to directly affect its own fate and that of most of the other species on this planet.[18] We are indeed recklessly gambling with the future of our common home. As Seán McDonagh writes, "The stakes are very high. In fact, they could not be higher!"[19]

Pope Francis is critical of those who deny or remain indifferent to the crisis of our common home. He judges such attitudes to be grossly irresponsible:

As often occurs in periods of deep crisis which require bold decisions, we are tempted to think that what is happening is not entirely clear. Superficially, apart from a few obvious

17. The Geological Society, *Climate Change: Evidence from the Geological Record; A Statement from the Geological Society of London* (November 2010), 7.

18. See Paul Ehrlich and Robert M. Pringle, "Where Does Biodiversity Go from Here? A Grim Business-as-usual Forecast and a Hopeful Portfolio of Partial Solutions," *Proceedings of the National Academy of Sciences* 105 (2008), 11579.

19. Seán McDonagh, *On Care for Our Common Home* Laudato Si': *The Encyclical of Pope Francis on the Environment* (New York: Orbis, 2016), 142.

signs of pollution and deterioration, things do not look that
serious, and the planet could continue as it is for some time.
Such evasiveness serves as a licence to carrying on with
our present lifestyles and models of production and consumption. This is the way human beings contrive to feed
their self-destructive vices: trying not to see them, trying
not to acknowledge them, delaying the important decisions
and pretending that nothing will happen. (59)

Against the alarming situation of our common planetary
home, Pope Francis asks emphatically: "What kind of world
do we want to leave to those who come after us, to children
who are now growing up?" As the pope notes, "leaving an
uninhabitable planet to future generations" is indeed a dreadful heritage that our present generation may end up with
(160).

Doomsday predictions can no longer be met with irony or
disdain. We may well be leaving the coming generations
debris, desolation and filth. The pace of consumption, waste
and environmental change has so stretched the planet's capacity that our contemporary lifestyle, unsustainable as it is,
can only precipitate catastrophes, such as those which even
now periodically occur in different areas of the world (161).

Our common home is in grave peril today. *Laudato Si'* is
therefore precisely about "care for our common home."

GREEN COMMANDMENT II
Listen to the Cry of the Poor

The second green commandment invites us to hear the cry of the poor who are the disproportionate victims of the degradation of our common home. One of the important contributions that Pope Francis makes in the encyclical is to integrate the concerns of the planet and of the poor. He reminds us that ecological crisis is not so much talk about the extinction of polar bears and exotic pandas, but about the plight of millions of our less fortunate brothers and sisters, members of our common household. According to Pope Francis, "Today, however, we have to realize that a true ecological approach *always* becomes a social approach; it must integrate questions of justice in debates on the environment, so as to hear *both the cry of the earth and the cry of the poor*" (49). The contemporary ecological crisis is not just a physical problem but is also a profoundly moral crisis as Pope John Paul II had noted already in 1990.[1] It is so precisely for the disproportionate impacts of the crisis on poor people and communities around the world. The cry of the earth thus becomes also a cry of the poor and calls out for eco-justice.

---

1. Pope John Paul II, *Peace with God the Creator, Peace with All of Creation* (Message for the World Day of Peace, 1 January 1990), nn. 7–8, 15.

In this section, we shall see, first of all, how the poor members of our human family are the main victims of the deterioration of our common home. The disproportionate effect of ecological degradation on the poor and on the developing world is highlighted in almost every section of *Laudato Si'*. Pope Francis looks at the crisis of our common home from the vantage point of the poor who are its worst victims. Secondly, we will discuss how the encyclical links the cry of the earth and the cry of the poor. The pope is particularly attentive to the vulnerable victims of the ecological crisis like women, indigenous communities, and future generations. Third, we will discuss the question of eco-justice raised by the encyclical. At the heart of the contemporary ecological crisis is a profound ethical dilemma due to the fact that the harm to our common home, as in the case of climate change, is caused largely by the rich, but its early and disproportionate victims are the poor and vulnerable members of our common human family. The pope speaks in this regard of the ecological debt that the developed world owes to the poorer nations and communities around the world.

The Crisis of Our Common Home from the Perspective of the Poor

In *Laudato Si'*, Pope Francis looks at the crisis of our common home from different perspectives: scientific, religious, economic, political, cultural, and so on. However, there is one perspective that stands out conspicuously. It is the ethical perspective and that too from the vantage point of poor and vulnerable persons and communities. Pope Francis looks at the ecological crisis from the "underside of history,"[2] from

2. We may recall in this regard Gustavo Gutiérrez's important article: "Theology from the Underside of History," in *The Power of the Poor in History: Selected Writings* (London: SCM Press, 1983), 169–221.

the viewpoint of its disproportionate victims. "A preferential option for the poorest of our brothers and sisters . . . is in fact an ethical imperative essential for effectively attaining the common good" (158).

It is noteworthy that while outlining the major and recurring themes of the encyclical in the introduction (16), Pope Francis enumerates "the intimate relationship between the poor and the fragility of the planet" as the very first among them. Significantly, such a concern is mentioned also in the closing paragraph of the encyclical, as we read in the concluding prayer, "the poor and the earth are crying out" (240). The prominence awarded to this question is not just casual. The concern for the poor—and as the pope mentions "the earth herself, burdened and laid waste, is among the most abandoned and maltreated of our poor" (2)—is at the heart of the encyclical and, as it is evident by now, at the heart of Pope Francis's own personal vision and universal mission. *Laudato Si'* is, in fact, more a social encyclical than one on climate change. *Climate* is mentioned just fourteen times in the text, while *the poor*, fifty-nine times,[3] significantly almost as many times as the word *creation* which appears sixty-six times.[4]

In the first chapter of the encyclical, Pope Francis follows up the description of the alarming state of our common home on account of pollution, climate change, depletion of natural resources, and loss of biodiversity with the equally worrying situation of the concrete living surroundings of many of our fellow sisters and brothers around the world. He speaks of the dehumanizing urban landscapes and of the uninhabitable

---

3. See Mike Hulme, "Finding the Message of the Pope's Encyclical," *Environment Science and Policy for Sustainable Development* 57/6 (2015), 17.

4. Maria Teresa Davila, "The Option for the Poor in *Laudato Si'*: Connecting Care of Creation with Care for the Poor," in *The Theological and Ecological Vision of Laudato Si': Everything Is Connected*, ed. Vincent J. Miller, 149 (London: Bloomsbury, 2017).

conditions of many of our cities where the poor people, "the disposable of society live" (45).

> We are conscious of the disproportionate and unruly growth of many cities, which have become unhealthy to live in, not only because of pollution caused by toxic emissions but also as a result of urban chaos, poor transportation, and visual pollution and noise. Many cities are huge, inefficient structures, excessively wasteful of energy and water. Neighbourhoods, even those recently built, are congested, chaotic and lacking in sufficient green space. We were not meant to be inundated by cement, asphalt, glass and metal, and deprived of physical contact with nature. (44)

Pope Francis is quick to note that "the deterioration of the environment and of society affects the most vulnerable people on the planet" (48). The pope drives home this message citing from the pastoral letters of the Bolivian and German bishops.

"Both everyday experience and scientific research show that the gravest effects of all attacks on the environment are suffered by the poorest."[5] For example, the depletion of fishing reserves especially hurts small fishing communities without the means to replace those resources; water pollution particularly affects the poor who cannot buy bottled water; and rises in the sea level mainly affect impoverished coastal populations who have nowhere else to go. The impact of present imbalances is also seen in the premature death of many of the poor, in conflicts sparked by the shortage of re-

---

5. Bolivian Bishops' Conference, Pastoral Letter on the Environment and Human Development in Bolivia *El universo, don de Dios para la vida* (23 March 2012), 17.

sources, and in any number of other problems which are insufficiently represented on global agendas[6] (48).

The pope decries the fact that on the global arena "there is little in the way of clear awareness of problems which especially affect the excluded" (49). The poor are conveniently forgotten or ignored at the High Table of world affairs. Yet, as the pope points out, "They are the majority of the planet's population, billions of people" (49). The pope speaks in very powerful terms of the amnesia or negligence of the poor on the part of the rich and powerful minority elite who are at the helm of world economy and politics:

> Indeed, when all is said and done, they [the poor] frequently remain at the bottom of the pile. This is due partly to the fact that many professionals, opinion makers, communications media and centres of power, being located in affluent urban areas, are far removed from the poor, with little direct contact with their problems. They live and reason from the comfortable position of a high level of development and a quality of life well beyond the reach of the majority of the world's population. (49)

The Cry of the Earth and the Cry of the Poor

The precarious state of our planetary home has a disastrous effect on vulnerable human communities. Pope Francis is truly concerned that the crisis has its worst impact on the poor. This is evident when he discusses pollution, the very first of the ecological questions addressed in the encyclical: "Exposure to atmospheric pollutants produces a broad spectrum of

6. Cf. German Bishops' Conference, Commission for Social Issues, *Der Klimawandel: Brennpunkt globaler, intergenerationeller und ökologischer Gerechtigkeit* (September 2006), 28–30.

health hazards, especially for the poor, and causes millions of premature deaths. People take sick, for example, from breathing high levels of smoke from fuels used in cooking or heating" (20). It is moving to note how attentive the pope is to the multitude of poor families around the world who use firewood or coal for cooking and heating, with disastrous effects on their health.

Pope Francis gives special attention to the consequences of global climate change on the poor, writing that "the poor live in areas particularly affected by phenomena related to warming, and their means of subsistence are largely dependent on natural reserves and ecosystemic services such as agriculture, fishing and forestry. They have no other financial activities or resources which can enable them to adapt to climate change or to face natural disasters, and their access to social services and protection is very limited" (25).

The encyclical unmasks the moral travesty of global climate change. The poor have benefited least from fossil fuels and are first in line to suffer as the effects of global warming intensify. It is known that the world's poor contribute virtually nothing to global warming. According to Partha Dasgupta and Veerabhadran Ramanathan, the top "1 billion people are responsible for 50% of greenhouse gas emissions; a further 3 billion people for 45%; while the bottom 3 billion, who do not have access to affordable fossil fuels, are responsible for a mere 5%."[7] As the authors rightly point out, "Although we all will soon be affected by climate change, it is the latter 3 billion who will, tragically, experience the worst consequences. Not only is their direct reliance on natural capital disproportionately large, they are also far less able to afford

7. Partha Dasgupta and Veerabhadran Ramanathan, "Pursuit of the Common Good: Religious Institutions May Mobilize Public Opinion and Action," *Science* 345 (19 September 2014), 1457.

protection from extreme weather events."[8] In the encyclical, the pope notes with sadness that while the worst impacts of climate change fall on the poorest, "many of those who possess more resources and economic and political power seem mostly to be concerned with masking the problems or concealing their symptoms" (26).

While discussing the impacts of climate change, Pope Francis is particularly attentive to the plight of "climate migrants" who are not protected by international conventions but whose numbers are constantly on the rise:

> There has been a tragic rise in the number of migrants seeking to flee from the growing poverty caused by environmental degradation. They are not recognized by international conventions as refugees; they bear the loss of the lives they have left behind, without enjoying any legal protection whatsoever. Sadly, there is widespread indifference to such suffering, which is even now taking place throughout our world. Our lack of response to these tragedies involving our brothers and sisters points to the loss of that sense of responsibility for our fellow men and women upon which all civil society is founded. (25)

Pope Francis's concern for the impact of the ecological crisis on the poor is equally evident when he discusses the question of water scarcity. He speaks of access to potable water as an issue of "primary" importance, though it is one rarely thought about in rich countries (28). "One particularly serious problem is the quality of water available to the poor. Every day, unsafe water results in many deaths and the spread of water-related diseases, including those caused by microorganisms and chemical substances. Dysentery and cholera, linked to inadequate

8. Ibid.

hygiene and water supplies, are a significant cause of suffering and of infant mortality" (29).

Pope Francis raises his voice in defense of some particular groups who are disproportionate victims of the crisis of our common home. One such group is the indigenous communities:

> In this sense, it is essential to show special care for indigenous communities and their cultural traditions. They are not merely one minority among others, but should be the principal dialogue partners, especially when large projects affecting their land are proposed. . . . When they remain on their land, they themselves care for it best. Nevertheless, in various parts of the world, pressure is being put on them to abandon their homelands to make room for agricultural or mining projects which are undertaken without regard for the degradation of nature and culture. (146)

Another group who will disproportionately incur the costs of the current ecological degradation are the future generations. Pope Francis warns that "we may well be leaving the coming generations debris, desolation and filth" (161). He is also clear that leaving an uninhabitable home to them (160) by the present generation is grossly immoral.

Ecological Debt:
Linking Social Justice and Environmental Justice

Laudato Si' connects the dots between social justice and environmental justice. Pope Francis reminds us that we need to "integrate questions of justice in debates on the environment" (49). According to him, "the mindset which leaves no room for sincere concern for the environment is the same mindset which lacks for the inclusion of the most vulnerable members of society" (196).

The sad paradox about the contemporary ecological crisis is that it is caused mainly by the rich minority, but its early, innocent, and disproportionate victims are the poor and vulnerable members of our common family. Such a realization necessitates that the ecological crisis be looked at from a justice angle. Pope Francis raises several instances of ecological and social injustices in our present world. The most important among them is the question of "ecological debt." Such a debt is incurred by the exploitation and unequal consumption of natural resources on the part of rich communities and by the disproportionate emission of greenhouse gases leading to global warming and associated climate change.

> A true "ecological debt" exists, particularly between the global north and south, connected to commercial imbalances with effects on the environment, and the disproportionate use of natural resources by certain countries over long periods of time. The export of raw materials to satisfy markets in the industrialized north has caused harm locally, as for example in mercury pollution in gold mining or sulphur dioxide pollution in copper mining. . . . The warming caused by huge consumption on the part of some rich countries has repercussions on the poorest areas of the world, especially Africa, where a rise in temperature, together with drought, has proved devastating for farming. (51)

As Christian Aid has pointed out, for their disproportionate contribution to the causes of climate change and its adverse effects, developed countries owe a twofold climate debt:

> For over-using and substantially diminishing the Earth's capacity to absorb greenhouse gases—denying it to the developing countries that most need it in the course of their development—the developed countries have run an "emissions debt" to developing countries. For the adverse effects of these excessive emissions—contributing to the escalating

losses, damages and lost development opportunities facing developing countries have run up an "adaptation debt" to developing countries. The sum of these debts—emissions debt and adaptation debt—constitutes the "climate debt" of developed countries.[9]

Climate change needs to be seen also through the prism of personal responsibility. While the historical responsibility for climate change is derived from the past emissions of greenhouse gases on the part of nations, the personal responsibility for climate change is evident in the current per capita emissions of individuals. The per capita emissions of greenhouse gases from individuals show a profoundly unjust and scandalous disparity. It should also be remembered that such emission patterns are totally unsustainable for the carrying capacity of our home planet's atmosphere. If every person living in the developing world had the same carbon footprint as the average for high income countries, we would require the atmospheres of six planets. With a global per capita carbon footprint at Australian levels, we would need seven planets, and with per capita footprint of Canada and United States we would require the atmospheres of nine planets![10]

The insistence on the personal responsibility of individual citizens for the crisis of our common home is important for yet another reason. There are vast differences in emission and consumption levels within the same nations, both rich and poor. With regard to climate change, for example, some developing countries have their elite who are very high emitters, while in the developed countries there are persons who are low emitters and desperately poor. The rich who overconsume Earth's resources and overpollute its common atmosphere are

9. Christian Aid, *Community Answers to Climate Chaos: Getting Climate Justice from the UNFCCC* (September 2009), 9.

10. United Nations Development Programme, *Human Development Report 2007/2008*, 48.

not limited to the developed world alone. The divide between the poor and the super-rich is conspicuous in most of the developing countries. In the city of Mumbai, the financial capital of India, the twenty-seven-story sprawling house of billionaire Mukesh Ambani sits uncomfortably nearby Asia's largest slum, Dharavi, with open sewers and crammed huts, home to more than a million people. Ultimately, the responsibility for the ecological crisis comes down to communities, households, and individuals who constitute the human society. In the case of climate change, for example, the problem is basically caused by the high emission rates of approximately 1 billion high emitters of our common household. Significantly, a scientific study led by Shoibal Chakravarty of Princeton University has shown how global projected emissions can be drastically reduced by engaging the 1.13 billion high emitters.[11]

Another mechanism to measure "ecological debt" is the "ecological footprint" of nations and individuals. The ecological footprint is an indicator of human pressure on the physical world in terms of humanity's consumption of natural resources, use of ecological services, and production of pollution and waste. There exist huge disparities in the consumption of natural resources across the globe that reveal scandalous differences in the ecological footprint of individuals and communities. The 2012 *Living Planet Report* gives some examples of the discrepancy in the ecological footprint of citizens around the globe:

> If all of humanity lived like an average Indonesian, for example, only two-thirds of the planet's biocapacity would be used; if everyone lived like an average Argentinian, humanity would demand more than half an additional planet; and if everyone lived like an average resident of

11. See Shoibal Chakravarty et al., "Sharing Global CO_2 Emission Reductions among One Billion High Emitters," *Proceedings of the National Academy of Sciences* 106 (2009), 11884–11888.

the USA, a total of four Earths would be required to regen-
erate humanity's annual demand on nature.[12]

The ecological footprint analysis reveals how the overconsumption of a small minority of our home planet's common
resources imperils our common home and especially the more
vulnerable members of our common household. It also manifests the ecological apartheid we live with, with the rich and
affluent plundering Earth's resources while the poor struggle
to meet their daily needs. The great ethical tragedy about the
contemporary ecological crisis is that a large majority of the
members of our common household suffer on account of the
greedy actions of a minority. As denounced by the Brazilian
Archbishop Helder Camara, the ecological crisis is caused
because "greedy or thoughtless people destroy what belongs
to all."[13]

Eco-Justice: A Common but Differentiated Responsibility

In the context of the current ecological crisis, all of humanity
needs to work together to avert the crisis, as it is the common
home of the Earth which is in peril. While all have a *common*
responsibility toward the current state of the planet and need
to work together to save it, such a responsibility, however, is at
the same time *differentiated*, in terms of one's past and present
responsibilities and current financial and technical capabilities
within the overall framework of justice, equity, and solidarity.

With regard to climate change negotiations in particular,
Pope Francis reiterates the principle of "differentiated respon-

12. Global Footprint Network et al., *Living Planet Report 2012: Biodiversity, Biocapacity and Better Choices* (Gland: WWF, 2012), 43.

13. Helder Camara, *Sister Earth: Creation, Ecology and the Spirit* (New
York: New City Press, 2008), 7.

sibilities" when it comes to the question of policies to be adopted by nations for the mitigation of anthropogenic climate change (52). When it comes to the rights of future emissions of greenhouse gases, the pope affirms that "there is a pressing need to calculate the use of environmental space throughout the world for depositing gas residues which have been accumulating for two centuries and have created a situation which currently affects all the countries of the world" (51). The pope is critical of those strategies for reduction of greenhouse gases that unduly penalize the poor:

> Some strategies for lowering pollutant gas emissions call for the internationalization of environmental costs, which would risk imposing on countries with fewer resources burdensome commitments to reducing emissions comparable to those of the more industrialized countries. Imposing such measures penalizes those countries most in need of development. A further injustice is perpetrated under the guise of protecting the environment. Here also, the poor end up paying the price. (170)

Pope Francis therefore calls for "common and differentiated responsibilities"—a principle long enshrined in the *United Nations Framework Convention on Climate Change*—in humanity's response to the crisis of our common home. "As the bishops of Bolivia have stated, 'the countries which have benefited from a high degree of industrialization, at the cost of enormous emissions of greenhouse gases, have a greater responsibility for providing a solution to the problems they have caused.'"[14] (170).

14. Bolivian Bishops' Conference, Pastoral Letter on the Environment and Human Development in Bolivia *El universo, don de Dios para la vida* (March 2012), 86.

An important pillar on which eco-justice needs to be erected is that of equity.[15] The principle of equity is based on the foundational value of human equality and dignity, namely, that all persons are born equal and have equal rights to the resources of our home planet, our common habitat (*oikos*), and to its common atmosphere. The fact of living in our common home and being members of our common human family confers on each human person the right to equal ecological space. Accordingly, "the Earth's atmosphere is a common resource without borders,"[16] to which all have equal rights, precisely in being members of the common household. As the Earth's ability to absorb greenhouse gases is a "global common," it is vital this global common should be shared equally.[17] It is the truth of global commons, namely, that our home planet and its common atmosphere, ecosystems, and natural resources are "common goods," which belong to all. As Pope Paul VI wrote, "God intended the Earth and everything in it for the use of all human beings and peoples. . . . Created goods should flow fairly to all."[18] Pope Francis considers "the notion of the common good, a central and unifying principle of social ethics" (156) and sees climate, for example, as a "common good" (23–26).

In order to truly achieve eco-justice for all the members of our common household "we need to strengthen the conviction that we are one single human family" (52). Pope Francis speaks eloquently of solidarity and the preferential option

15. See Joshtrom Isaac Kureethadam, *Creation in Crisis: Science, Ethics, Theology* (New York: Orbis, 2014), 278–79.

16. United Nations Development Programme, *Human Development Report 2007/08*, 39.

17. Anil Agarwal and Sunita Narain, *Global Warming in An Unequal World: A Case of Environmental Colonialism* (New Delhi: Centre for Science and Environment, 1991), 13.

18. Pope Paul VI, Encyclical Letter *Populorum Progressio*, n. 22.

for the poor as the best means to attain common good and build eco-justice:

> In the present condition of global society, where injustices abound and growing numbers of people are deprived of basic human rights and considered expendable, the principle of the common good immediately becomes, logically and inevitably, a summons to solidarity and a preferential option for the poorest of our brothers and sisters. This option entails recognizing the implications of the universal destination of the world's goods. . . . It demands before all else an appreciation of the immense dignity of the poor in the light of our deepest convictions as believers. We need only look around us to see that, today, this option is in fact an ethical imperative essential for effectively attaining the common good. (158)

The contemporary ecological crisis is indeed a profoundly moral crisis and we all have a moral imperative to care for our common home and for the most vulnerable members of our common household. This is certainly one of the central pillars of *Laudato Si'* and of Catholic social doctrine. The encyclical clearly reveals how the crisis of our common home is not just a physical one but also a profoundly moral one, calling for eco-justice. The question of eco-justice is indeed one of the main challenges, unpleasant as it may be, raised by the encyclical. Pope Francis speaks on behalf of the poor and vulnerable, becoming a clear voice for the multitude of voiceless victims of the crisis of our common home. According to him, "every ecological approach needs to incorporate a social perspective which takes into account the fundamental rights of the poor and the underprivileged" (93).

The crisis of our common home is one of the greatest ethical dilemmas of our time on account of the stark injustice and inequity masked by it. At the same time, the silver lining in the clouds is that acting against it in the spirit of solidarity, humanity has also a precious opportunity to create a more equitable and just world. *Laudato Si'* is a loud clarion call in this regard. The pope also invites us to pray for the grace to become responsible stewards of the earth and of the poor. He writes in the first of the concluding prayers to the encyclical:

> O God of the poor,
> help us to rescue the abandoned
> and forgotten of this earth,
> so precious in your eyes.
> Bring healing to our lives,
> that we may protect the world and not prey on it,
> that we may sow beauty,
> not pollution and destruction. (246)

PART TWO: JUDGING

(Discerning the Crisis of Our Common Home)

GREEN COMMANDMENT III

Rediscover a Theological Vision
of the Natural World

GREEN COMMANDMENT IV

Recognize That the Abuse of Creation
Is Ecological Sin

GREEN COMMANDMENT V

Acknowledge the Human Roots of the Crisis
of Our Common Home

We are reading Laudato Si', Pope Francis's encyclical on care for our common home, within the see-judge-act methodology. The first two green commandments, corresponding to the first chapter of the encyclical, offer us an understanding of the ecological crisis as the cry of the earth and the cry of the poor. The next three green commandments will attempt to "judge" the crisis of our common home. It is precisely the intermediary moment of discernment which needs to follow our understanding of the problem and precede our attempts to resolve it. We will base ourselves in this phase mainly, though not exclusively, on the third and fourth chapters of the encyclical.

The third green commandment presents the theological criterion offered by Pope Francis to judge the crisis of our common home. In Laudato Si', the pope invites us to see the world from a religious perspective. The encyclical presents the natural world as the Gospel (good news) of creation, an expression of God's infinite love for every creature. Creation is also the primordial revelation of God, the "Book of Works." It is also important to remember that God has oriented creation for universal communion, and earthly goods therefore belong to all. Creation's ultimate destiny is to be recapitulated in Christ. The pope invites us to see the natural world with Jesus' own gaze on creation.

Our judgment of the crisis reveals that the abuse of the natural world on the part of humanity is nothing less than sinful behavior. The fourth green commandment is therefore about the concept of ecological sin. We are invited, first of all, to widen our traditional understanding of sin, often couched in individualistic categories. Pope Francis offers a rather holistic understanding of ecological sin as the rupture of basic relationships with the Creator, with fellow human beings, and with the rest of creation. We will therefore seek to show the triple layers of ecological sin *that ruptures the bonds of divine, human, and cosmic fellowship. We will then reflect on the repercussions of human sin on the rest of creation and conclude with a note on the need for repentance and reconciliation.*

A process of genuine discernment regarding the crisis of our common home leads us to unearth and acknowledge the root causes of the problem. The fifth green commandment is thus about the human roots of the ecological crisis, which is also the title of the third chapter of the encyclical. Here we are concerned with owning up to our responsibility for the defilement of our common home, a prerequisite for any effective response to the crisis. Pope Francis begins with a reflection on the current technocratic paradigm which has led to the mastery and pillage of the natural world. However, he is quick to note that underlying the technocratic approach are the deeper roots of the ecological crisis, namely, modern anthropocentrism and a mechanistic perception of the natural world merely as a storehouse of resources. The pope speaks of a conceptual paradigm change required to overcome the ideological roots of the current degradation of our common home.

GREEN COMMANDMENT III

Rediscover a Theological Vision of the Natural World

Chapter 2 of *Laudato Si'* is significantly entitled "The Gospel of Creation" and presents the theological foundations of the encyclical's ecological vision.[1] Pope Francis, true to his vocation as a spiritual leader, offers a theological criteria to judge the crisis of our common home. In the third green commandment, we shall reflect on the religious vision of the natural world offered by Pope Francis.

We will begin by reflecting on the importance of a theological perspective on the contemporary ecological crisis. We will then present the "good news" (Gospel) of creation offered in the encyclical. Creation is good news for two fundamental reasons. First of all, creation is very good in God's own eyes, as we read in the creation narrative in the book of Genesis. Secondly, creation is a profound act of love on the part of God. On a deeper level, creation is the primordial revelation of God, as it is God's "Book of Works." God has oriented creation for universal communion, and earthly goods therefore belong to all. Creation's ultimate destiny is to be recapitulated in Christ.

---

1. Susan Rakoczy, "The Mission Spirituality of *Laudato Si'*: Ecological Conversion and the World Church," *Grace & Truth* 34 (2017), 68.

We will conclude our overview of the theological vision of the
encyclical with Jesus' own gaze on creation.

The Theology of Laudato Si': *Creation as "Good News"*

Pope Francis considers a theological perspective on the contemporary ecological crisis vitally important and offers an apol-
ogy about it right at the beginning of the second chapter of
Laudato Si'. He asks in the very opening sentence, "Why should
this document, addressed to all people of good will, include a
chapter dealing with the convictions of believers?" (62). He
himself provides the answer in the very next paragraph:

> Given the complexity of the ecological crisis and its mul-
> tiple causes, we need to realize that the solutions will not
> emerge from just one way of interpreting and transforming
> reality. Respect must also be shown for the various cultural
> riches of different peoples, their art and poetry, their inte-
> rior life and spirituality. If we are truly concerned to de-
> velop an ecology capable of remedying the damage we
> have done, no branch of the sciences and no form of wis-
> dom can be left out, and that includes religion and the
> language particular to it. (63)

In dedicating an entire chapter to the religious perspective
on the natural world in *Laudato Si'*, Pope Francis recovers
much lost ground on the part of faith traditions on the urgent
question of the degradation of our planetary home. The pope
affirms that the ecological crisis is not only about the collapse
of the planet's ecosystems and biochemical cycles with a profound impact on human populations, especially on the poor,
but is also ultimately a theological issue. The ecological crisis
is not only a physical problem and a moral predicament. It is,

in fact, symptomatic of a deeper spiritual crisis.[2] The contemporary ecological crisis points to the *amnesia* (forgetfulness) of a deeper truth, namely, that the physical world is above all God's creation and is permeated with the divine presence.[3]

As Denis Edwards writes, "One of the key contributions of *Laudato Si'* to contemporary theology, and to Christian ecological practice, is its theology of the natural world."[4] The theology of Earth presented in *Laudato Si'* is a vital tool to understand the ecological crisis and to respond to it effectively. It is to a detailed presentation of the theological understanding of the natural world offered in the encyclical that we now turn our attention.

The very title of the second chapter of *Laudato Si'*, wherein Pope Francis offers the theological vision of the natural world, is highly significant. The chapter carries the title "The Gospel of Creation." The encyclical affirms that creation is truly Gospel, *evangelion*, that is, "good news."[5] In the wake of modernity, we have been accustomed to look at the natural world as inert matter—the Cartesian *res extensa*, as in modern science, or as merely a storehouse of resources, as in the neoliberal economy. The encyclical instead reminds us of a

2. See Andrea Cohen-Kiener, *Claiming Earth as Common Ground: The Ecological Crisis through the Lens of Faith* (Woodstock, VT: Skylight Paths, 2009), 2; Dave Bookless, *Planet Wise: Dare to Care for God's World* (Nottingham: Inter-Varsity Press, 2008), 41.

3. See Joshtrom Isaac Kureethadam, *Creation in Crisis: Science, Ethics, Theology* (New York: Orbis, 2014), 288–91.

4. Denis Edwards, " 'Everything Is Interconnected': The Trinity and the Natural World in *Laudato Si'*," *The Australasian Catholic Record* 94 (2017), 83.

5. The etymological root of the Greek word *evangelion* is the verb ἀγγέλλω (*angello*) which means "to announce" or "to bring news of" plus the prefix εὐ (*eu*) which simply means "good" or "well." Thus *evangelion* means good news.

fundamental truth of Christian faith that the natural world is above all creation and, as such, is "good news." *Laudato Si'* is radical not only as social teaching but also as theology of creation. According to Carmody Grey, with the phrase "Gospel of creation" alone, Pope Francis "inaugurates a new era in the Catholic Church's approach to the natural world. The world of animals, forests, mountains and waters are inextricably part of God's good news for us; they express and participate in the mystery of salvation."[6]

Creation is good news on account of two fundamental truths about it. First of all, creation has a basic goodness about it as we read in the book of Genesis. Secondly, the physical world has been brought into existence as an act of love on the part of the triune God. We shall reflect on both these elements in the light of the teachings of the encyclical.

For a believer, it is the basic goodness of creation in God's own eyes that constitutes the intrinsic worth of every created reality. If God created the world, then the world and everything in it, including all forms of animate and inanimate matter, must have value. According to Pope Francis, "Each organism, as a creature of God, is good and admirable in itself; the same is true of the harmonious ensemble of organisms existing in a defined space and functioning as a system" (140). We are invited therefore to recognize the "divine dignity" of every created being. As the encyclical states:

> We are called to recognize that other living beings have a value of their own in God's eyes: "by their mere existence they bless him and give him glory,"[7] and indeed, "the Lord rejoices in all his works" (Ps 104:31). . . . The Catechism clearly and forcefully criticizes a distorted anthropocentrism: "Each creature possesses its own particular goodness

6. Carmody Grey, "Walk with the Animals," *The Tablet* (4 July 2015), 11.
7. *Catechism of the Catholic Church*, 2416.

and perfection. . . . Each of the various creatures, willed
in its own being, reflects in its own way a ray of God's
infinite wisdom and goodness. Man must therefore respect
the particular goodness of every creature, to avoid any
disordered use of things."[8] (69)

Since "the earth is the Lord's" (Ps 24:1) and to him belongs
"the earth with all that is within it" (Deut 10:14), it is clear that
we are not proprietors of the earth. "The earth was here before
us and has been given to us." This fundamental realization
"allows us to respond to the charge that Judaeo-Christian
thinking, on the basis of the Genesis account which grants
man 'dominion' over the earth (cf. *Gen* 1:28), has encouraged
the unbridled exploitation of nature by painting him as domi-
neering and destructive by nature"[9] (67). The pope states
clearly that "this is not a correct interpretation of the Bible as
understood by the Church" and adds that "we must forcefully
reject the notion that our being created in God's image and
given dominion over the earth justifies absolute domination
over other creatures" (67).

Pope Francis reminds us that the command to humanity
is to "till and keep" the garden of the world (see Gen 2:15).
"Tilling" refers to cultivating, ploughing or working, while
"keeping" means caring, protecting, overseeing, and preserving (67). The pope is keen to point out that "clearly, the Bible
has no place for a tyrannical anthropocentrism unconcerned
for other creatures" (68). As such, we have no "right to tram-
ple his creation underfoot" (75). Pope Francis clearly affirms
that "thus God rejects every claim to absolute ownership: The

8. Ibid., 339.
9. The encyclical here responds to the famous article of Lynn White
Jr. in 1967 which laid the blame for our environmental crisis largely on
Christianity. See Lynn White Jr., "The Historic Roots of our Ecologic
Crisis," *Science* 155 (1967), 1203–7.

land shall not be sold in perpetuity, for the land is mine; for you are strangers and sojourners with me (*Lev* 25:23)" (67). According to the pope, "the best way to restore men and women to their rightful place, putting an end to their claim to absolute dominion over the earth, is to speak once more of the figure of a Father who creates and who alone owns the world. Otherwise, human beings will always try to impose their own laws and interests on reality" (75).

The second fundamental truth about creation is that it is a love story on the part of God. Creation is an act of God's love, realized in total freedom. Our physical universe is not an accident, or a fluke event, as it is sometimes presumed in secular thought and culture. Pope Francis notes that within the Judaeo-Christian tradition, "the word 'creation' has a broader meaning than 'nature,' for it has to do with God's loving plan in which every creature has its own value and significance" (76). For this reason, unlike a detached study of nature, "creation can only be understood as a gift from the outstretched hand of the Father of all, and as a reality illuminated by the love which calls us together into universal communion" (76).

The whole of creation and every creature is a sign of God's outpouring love. "In contrast to the violent beginning motifs of pagan cosmogonies, the Bible depicts creation as the tender loving act of a gracious God."[10] Pope Francis states: "The universe did not emerge as the result of arbitrary omnipotence, a show of force or a desire for self-assertion. Creation is of the order of love. God's love is the fundamental moving force in all created things" (77). Every creature is brought into existence out of love and with a definite purpose. God's self-sharing love is what animates every creature:

---

10. Richard A. Young, *Healing the Earth: A Theocentric Perspective on Environmental Problems and Other Solutions* (Nashville: Broadman & Holman, 1994), 85.

Every creature is thus the object of the Father's tenderness, who gives it its place in the world. Even the fleeting life of the least of beings is the object of his love, and in its few seconds of existence, God enfolds it with his affection. Saint Basil the Great described the Creator as "goodness without measure,"[11] while Dante Alighieri spoke of "the love which moves."[12] (77)

Earth, our home planet, is thus the gift of a loving Creator, clasped intimately in his loving embrace. In rather poetic terms, the pope writes that "the entire material universe speaks of God's love, his boundless affection for us. Soil, water, mountains: everything is, as it were, a caress of God" (84). Creation is, indeed, a tangible expression of the triune God's outpouring of love. It is all the more in the case of humanity. In the last analysis, we owe our existence to the infinite love of the Creator who brought us into being and this "special love of the Creator for each human being," as John Paul II had pointed out, "confers upon him or her an infinite dignity"[13] (65). Pope Francis reminds us that we are not here by chance, that each of us has been willed and loved by God:

How wonderful is the certainty that each human life is not adrift in the midst of hopeless chaos, in a world ruled by pure chance or endlessly recurring cycles! The Creator can say to each one of us: "Before I formed you in the womb, I knew you" (*Jer* 1:5). We were conceived in the heart of

11. Basil the Great, *Hom. in Hexaemeron,* I, 2, 10: *PG* 29, 9.

12. Dante, *The Divine Comedy, Paradiso,* Canto XXXIII, 145. See in this regard Elizabeth T. Groppe, "'The Love that Moves the Sun and the Stars': A Theology of Creation," in *The Theological and Ecological Vision of Laudato Si': Everything Is Connected,* ed. Vincent J. Miller, 78–94 (London: Bloomsbury, 2017).

13. Pope John Paul II, *Angelus* in Osnabrück (Germany) with the disabled (16 November 1980), *Insegnamenti* 3/2 (1980), 1232.

God, and for this reason "each of us is the result of a thought of God. Each of us is willed, each of us is loved, each of us is necessary."[14] (65)

According to Pope Francis, the entire creation is "open to God's transcendence, within which it develops" (79). But God is not only transcendent to creation, but also deeply immanent in it. In this context, Pope Francis quotes the bishops of Brazil who "have pointed out that nature as a whole not only manifests God but is also a locus of his presence"[15] (88). God's immanent presence to every being in the physical universe is through the Holy Spirit who indwells and guides the whole of creation. Pope Francis writes:

> God is intimately present to each being, without impinging on the autonomy of his creature, and this gives rise to the rightful autonomy of earthly affairs.[16] His divine presence, which ensures the subsistence and growth of each being, "continues the work of creation."[17] The Spirit of God has filled the universe with possibilities and therefore, from the very heart of things, something new can always emerge: "Nature is nothing other than a certain kind of art, namely God's art, impressed upon things, whereby those things are moved to a determinate end. It is as if a shipbuilder were able to give timbers the wherewithal to move themselves to take the form of a ship."[18] (80)

---

14. Pope Benedict XVI, *Homily for the Solemn Inauguration of the Petrine Ministry* (24 April 2005): *AAS* 97 (2005), 711.

15. Cf. National Conference of the Bishops of Brazil, *A Igreja e a Questão Ecológica* (1992), 53–54.

16. Cf. Second Vatican Ecumenical Council, Pastoral Constitution on the Church in the Modern World *Gaudium et Spes*, 36.

17. Thomas Aquinas, *Summa Theologiae*, I, q. 104, art. 1, ad. 4.

18. Aquinas, *In octo libros Physicorum Aristotelis expositio*, Lib. II, lectio 14.

The constant and accompanying presence of the Spirit of God in creation is the ultimate guarantee of the fruitfulness of our efforts to care for our increasingly imperiled planetary home. "The Holy Spirit can be said to possess an infinite creativity, proper to the divine mind, which knows how to loosen the knots of human affairs, including the most complex and inscrutable"[19] (80).

Creation as God's Self-Revelation

Creation is God's first and primordial revelation.[20] According to Pope Francis, "God has written a precious book, 'whose letters are the multitude of created things present in the universe' "[21] (85). Creation is, indeed, the very first epiphany of God. Citing his predecessor Pope John Paul II, Pope Francis reminds us that "for the believer, to contemplate creation is to hear a message, to listen to a paradoxical and silent voice"[22]; and that "alongside revelation properly so-called, contained in sacred Scripture, there is a divine manifestation in the blaze of the sun and the fall of night"[23] (85).

Pope Francis quotes from the Pastoral Letter of the Canadian bishops to point out that no creature is excluded from this manifestation of God: "From panoramic vistas to the tiniest living form, nature is a constant source of wonder and awe.

19. John Paul II, *Catechesis* (24 April 1991), 6: *Insegnamenti* 14 (1991), 856.

20. See Kureethadam, *Creation in Crisis*, 306–11.

21. John Paul II, *Catechesis* (30 January 2002), 6: *Insegnamenti* 25/1 (2002), 140.

22. John Paul II, *Catechesis* (26 January 2000), 5: *Insegnamenti* 23/1 (2000), 123.

23. John Paul II, *Catechesis* (2 August 2000), 3: *Insegnamenti* 23/2 (2000), 112.

It is also a continuing revelation of the divine"[24] (85). He also quotes the bishops of Japan who "made a thought-provoking observation: 'To sense each creature singing the hymn of its existence is to live joyfully in God's love and hope.'[25] This contemplation of creation allows us to discover in each thing a teaching which God wishes to hand on to us" (85).

In *Laudato Si'*, Pope Francis returns often to the symbolic view of creation. Created realities are ultimately symbols of God. Creation's value lies precisely in its symbolism, in its capacity to link the finite with the infinite. As symbols of God, created realities are *vestigia Dei*, signs and traces of God's presence in creation. As Anthony Kelly explains, "The universe, created in the Word (*Logos*) is a world of endlessly differentiated 'words' (*logoi*) or meanings."[26] In this regard, Pope Francis points out in *Laudato Si'* that "each creature reflects something of God and has a message to convey to us" (221). Citing the *Catechism of the Catholic Church*, Francis writes that "each of the various creatures, willed in its own being, reflects in its own way a ray of God's infinite wisdom and goodness"[27] (69). Referring to the problem of species extinction earlier in the encyclical, Pope Francis notes with sadness and with profound theological insight, "Because of us, thousands of species will no longer give glory to God by their very existence, nor convey their message to us. We have no such right" (33).

---

24. Canadian Conference of Catholic Bishops, Social Affairs Commission, Pastoral Letter *You Love All that Exists. . . . All Things are Yours, God, Lover of Life* (4 October 2003), 1.

25. Catholic Bishops' Conference of Japan, *Reverence for Life: A Message for the Twenty-First Century* (1 January 2000), 89.

26. Anthony J. Kelly, *Laudato Si': An Integral Ecology and the Catholic Tradition* (Adelaide: ATF Theology, 2016), 92.

27. *Catechism of the Catholic Church*, 339.

In all religious traditions, there have been innumerable sages and holy men and women who were able to see God in the mirror of his creation and who were able to perceive creation and created realities as living symbols of God. In the Catholic tradition, the example of St. Francis of Assisi is probably the most illuminating in this regard. For the *poverello* of Assisi, every flower, every bird spoke to him of the Creator, of God. Pope Francis writes in *Laudato Si'*:

> Saint Francis, faithful to Scripture, invites us to see nature as a magnificent book in which God speaks to us and grants us a glimpse of his infinite beauty and goodness. "Through the greatness and the beauty of creatures one comes to know by analogy their maker" (*Wis* 13:5); indeed, "his eternal power and divinity have been made known through his works since the creation of the world" (*Rom* 1:20). For this reason, Francis asked that part of the friary garden always be left untouched, so that wild flowers and herbs could grow there, and those who saw them could raise their minds to God, the Creator of such beauty.[28] (12)

When created things become *vestigia Dei*, creation becomes a true act of communication. As in every act of communication, no single word or expression will be sufficient to communicate reality. It is also true of God's communication in creation. No one creature, not even the human, is sufficient to represent God. The infinitely diverse living species are indeed pages of God's great Book of Works, revealing the Creator's wisdom and goodness. The exuberance of creation thus represents the infinite fecundity of God. "The universe as a whole, in all its manifold relationships, shows forth the

---

28. Cf. Thomas of Celano, *The Remembrance of the Desire of a Soul*, II, 124, 165, in *Francis of Assisi: Early Documents*, vol. 2 (New York: New City Press, 2000), 354.

inexhaustible riches of God" (86). It was a point masterfully brought home to us by the thirteenth century medieval theologian Thomas Aquinas who argued that the diversity of the extraordinary array of creatures roaming the earth reveals the richness of the nature of God.

Saint Thomas Aquinas wisely noted that multiplicity and variety "come from the intention of the first agent" who willed that "what was wanting to one in the representation of the divine goodness might be supplied by another,"[29] inasmuch as God's goodness "could not be represented fittingly by any one creature."[30] Hence we need to grasp the variety of things in their multiple relationships.[31] We understand better the importance and meaning of each creature if we contemplate it within the entirety of God's plan (86).

Creation's Call to Universal Communion

Creation not only reveals and points to our symbolic communion with the Divine but is also a concrete means for communion within the human family and within the larger biotic community. Pope Francis speaks of this universal communion in *Laudato Si'*: "As part of the universe, called into being by one Father, all of us are linked by unseen bonds and together form a kind of universal family, a sublime communion which fills us with a sacred, affectionate and humble respect" (89). Pope Francis sees human life as a pilgrimage in communion along with the rest of God's creatures, bonded together by God's love. "Everything is related, and we human beings are united as brothers and sisters on a wonderful pilgrimage, woven together by the love God has for each of his creatures

29. *Summa Theologiae*, I, q. 47, art. 1.
30. Ibid.
31. Cf. Ibid., art. 2, ad. 1; art. 3.64.

and which also unites us in fond affection with brother sun, sister moon, brother river and mother earth" (92). It is precisely our profound communion with the wider earth community which makes us "feel the desertification of the soil almost as a physical ailment, and the extinction of a species as a painful disfigurement"[32] (89).

In *Laudato Si'*, Pope Francis also warns against possible aberrations in the realization of such a universal communion. He is especially critical of the tendency to deny any preeminence to the human person and show more zeal "in protecting other species than in defending the dignity which all human beings share in equal measure." The pope is also critical of the "enormous inequalities in our midst, whereby we continue to tolerate some considering themselves more worthy than others" which is totally against the truth of universal communion (90). We cannot live in communion with the natural world when we do not live in communion among ourselves:

> A sense of deep communion with the rest of nature cannot be real if our hearts lack tenderness, compassion and concern for our fellow human beings. It is clearly inconsistent to combat trafficking in endangered species while remaining completely indifferent to human trafficking, unconcerned about the poor, or undertaking to destroy another human being deemed unwanted. This compromises the very meaning of our struggle for the sake of the environment. (91)

The truth of the universal communion of the entire creation is the basis of a common fraternity "that excludes nothing and no one" (92). We cannot be at peace among ourselves, if

32. Pope Francis, Apostolic Exhortation *Evangelii Gaudium* (24 November 2013), 215: *AAS* 105 (2013), 1109. See in this regard Douglas E. Christie, "Becoming Painfully Aware: Spirituality and Solidarity in *Laudato Si'*," in *The Theological and Ecological Vision of Laudato Si'*, ed. Miller, 109–26.

we are not at peace with creation. With deep psychological insight, the pope writes, "We have only one heart, and the same wretchedness which leads us to mistreat an animal will not be long in showing itself in our relationships with other people" (92).

Our universal communion with the rest of the human family and with the whole of creation has concrete consequences. One of this is the "common destination" of all Earth's goods which "are meant to benefit everyone." Pope Francis reminds us that Pope John Paul II wrote in 1991, "God gave the earth to the whole human race for the sustenance of all its members, *without excluding or favouring anyone*"[33] (93). The common destination of earthly goods is also based on a profound theological truth. According to Pope Francis, the sharing of Earth's fruits is ultimately "a question of fidelity to the Creator, since God created the world for everyone" (93). As such, the common destination of goods is also an essential component of the church's social teachings.

> The principle of the subordination of private property to the universal destination of goods, and thus the right of everyone to their use, is a golden rule of social conduct and "the first principle of the whole ethical and social order."[34] The Christian tradition has never recognized the right to private property as absolute or inviolable, and has stressed the social purpose of all forms of private property. (93)

Citing Pope John Paul II, Pope Francis reminds us "that there is always a social mortgage on all private property, in order that goods may serve the general purpose that God

---

33. John Paul II, Encyclical Letter *Centesimus Annus* (1 May 1991), 31: *AAS* 83 (1991), 831.

34. John Paul II, Encyclical Letter *Laborem Exercens* (14 September 1981), 19: *AAS* 73 (1981), 626.

gave them"[35] (93). Therefore, "it is not in accord with God's plan that this gift be used in such a way that its benefits favour only a few"[36] (93).

Creation's ultimate destiny is the final communion with God, the Creator—the *telos* of all creation to be recapitulated in Christ when "God will be all in all." Pope Francis reminds us that "in the Christian understanding of the world, the destiny of all creation is bound up with the mystery of Christ, present from the beginning as 'all things have been created though him and for him' (*Col* 1:16)" (99). The pope writes, "The ultimate destiny of the universe is in the fullness of God, which has already been attained by the risen Christ, the measure of the maturity of all things" (83). It is important to remember that it is the whole of creation, the entire physical universe, and not just humanity alone, that is destined to be redeemed and transformed in Christ. Therefore, there is no reason for humans to tyrannically dominate other creatures. Rather, humanity's task is to lovingly accompany all of creation in their eschatological journey. We read in the encyclical:

> Here we can add yet another argument for rejecting every tyrannical and irresponsible domination of human beings over other creatures. The ultimate purpose of other creatures is not to be found in us. Rather, all creatures are moving forward with us and through us towards a common point of arrival, which is God, in that transcendent fullness where the risen Christ embraces and illumines all things. Human beings, endowed with intelligence and love, and drawn by the fullness of Christ, are called to lead all creatures back to their Creator. (83)

35. John Paul II, *Address to Indigenous and Rural People,* Cuilapán, Mexico (29 January 1979), 6: *AAS* 71 (1979), 209.

36. John Paul II, *Homily at Mass for Farmers,* Recife, Brazil (7 July 1980): *AAS* 72 (1980), 926.

From the perspective of Christian faith, the entire creation has an essentially christological dimension, as Christ is the Alpha and Omega of all created realities. We shall therefore conclude our presentation of the theological vision of the encyclical by dwelling on Jesus' own gaze on creation.

The Gaze of Jesus

Laudato Si' is about care for our common home. Earth is home not only for humanity and the rest of the biotic community. It is also God's home where the Word "became flesh and lived among us" (John 1:14). Among the billions and billions of celestial bodies in the universe, God chose to pitch his tent on this tiny planet, this "tiny blue dot" in the vast cosmic expanse, to say it with Carl Sagan. Earth, which had become a unique home for life through a process running into billions of years, becomes a home for life in abundance (John 10:10) in the person of God becoming a human being, Jesus Christ. "One Person of the Trinity entered into the created cosmos, throwing in his lot with it, even to the cross. From the beginning of the world, but particularly through the incarnation, the mystery of Christ is at work in a hidden manner in the natural world as a whole" (99). In the encyclical, Pope Francis highlights three elements of the gaze of "the earthly Jesus and his tangible and loving relationship with the world" (100). We shall briefly enumerate them below.

First of all, Jesus invited his disciples "to recognize the paternal relationship God has with all his creatures." He reminded them of the Father's loving tenderness and care for all creatures and how "each one of them is important in God's eyes: 'Are not five sparrows sold for two pennies? And not one of them is forgotten before God' (*Lk* 12:6). 'Look at the birds of the air: they neither sow nor reap nor gather into barns, and yet your heavenly Father feeds them' (*Mt* 6:26)" (96).

Secondly, the gaze of the earthly Jesus on creation was a contemplative one. According to the pope, Jesus "was able to invite others to be attentive to the beauty that there is in the world because he himself was in constant touch with nature, lending it an attention full of fondness and wonder. As he made his way throughout the land, he often stopped to contemplate the beauty sown by his Father, and invited his disciples to perceive a divine message in things" (97).

Third, "Jesus lived in full harmony with creation. . . . His appearance was not that of an ascetic set apart from the world, nor of an enemy to the pleasant things of life." Pope Francis points out that Jesus did not despise "the body, matter and the things of the world." For most of his life "Jesus worked with his hands, in daily contact with the matter created by God, to which he gave form by his craftsmanship" (98). He thus ennobled human work and, we might add, all human efforts to care for our common planetary home.

The earthly Jesus, risen and glorious, is "present throughout creation by his universal Lordship" (Col 1:19-20), reconciling to himself all things (100). As Pope Francis writes in the encyclical, "Christ has taken unto himself this material world and now, risen, is intimately present to each being, surrounding it with his affection and penetrating it with his light" (221). So we need "to direct our gaze to the end of time, when the Son will deliver all things to the Father, so that 'God may be everything to everyone' (*1 Cor* 15:28)" (100). The gaze of Jesus has profoundly transformed the whole of creation:

> Thus, the creatures of this world no longer appear to us under merely natural guise because the risen One is mysteriously holding them to himself and directing them towards fullness as their end. The very flowers of the field

and the birds which his human eyes contemplated and
admired are now imbued with his radiant presence. (100)

Creation is truly God's own *oikos* (house) as it is imbued
with the divine presence. The glory of God resounds throughout the universe in and through the risen Christ whose life
now flows throughout the cosmos through the life-giving
Spirit.

GREEN COMMANDMENT IV

Recognize That the Abuse of Creation Is Ecological Sin

An important contribution of *Laudato Si'* consists in having demonstrated the significant link between human sin and the precarious state of the physical world. The crisis of our common home is, in fact, only an externalization of a deeper inner malaise. As Pope Benedict XVI had pointed out, with a ring of prophecy, in the homily at the inaugural Mass of his pontificate in 2005, "The external deserts in the world are growing, because the internal deserts have become so vast."[1] Pope Francis recalls this affirmation (217) and mentions right at the beginning of his encyclical: "The violence present in our hearts, wounded by sin, is also reflected in the symptoms of sickness evident in the soil, in the water, in the air and in all forms of life" (2). The pope also notes how ubiquitous and pervasive is evil in "our situation today, where sin is manifest in all its destructive power in wars, the various forms of violence and abuse, the abandonment of the most vulnerable,

---

1. Pope Benedict XVI, *Homily for the Solemn Inauguration of the Petrine Ministry* (24 April 2005): *AAS* 97 (2005), 710.

and attacks on nature" (66). Sin distorts our understanding of ourselves and the world in which we live.[2]

Our fourth green commandment is about the concept of ecological sin. We will begin with a reflection on the need to widen our traditional understanding of sin couched largely in individualistic terms. In *Laudato Si'*, Pope Francis offers a holistic understanding of sin as the rupture of basic relationships: with the Creator, with our fellow human beings, and with creation itself. We will reflect on each of these interconnected layers and will reflect especially on the repercussions of human sin on the natural world. We will conclude by laying emphasis on the need for individual and collective repentance on the part of humanity in the context of the contemporary ecological crisis.

Ecological Sin as the Rupture of Relationships

In the context of the contemporary ecological crisis, we need to radically widen our understanding of the very concept of sin.[3] Traditionally, sin has been understood in a rather individualistic sense—as something limited to the personal sphere, concerning exclusively one's relationship with God. In recent times, there has been a greater critical awareness regarding the societal structures of sin and a condemnation of them in the teachings of the churches, including papal magisterium. Today, we need to broaden our understanding of sin within a planetary perspective. In fact, the crisis of our common home and the host of actions contributing to that crisis

---

2. See John Copeland Nagle, "Pope Francis, Environmental Anthropologist," *Regent University Law Review* 28/7 (2015–2016), 10.

3. See Joshtrom Isaac Kureethadam, *Creation in Crisis: Science, Ethics, Theology* (New York: Orbis, 2014), 338–40.

are best understood in the context of sin conceived within a much broader planetary perspective. Churches and religions are called today, in the context of the crisis of our common home, to widen their understanding of sin. John Zizioulas, the metropolitan of Pergamon, writes in this regard:

> The protection of the natural environment is a fundamental religious obligation demanded from humankind by God himself. This means that the Church will have to revise radically her concept of sin, which traditionally has been limited to the social and anthropological level, and start speaking of *sin against nature* as a matter of primary religious significance.[4]

Accordingly, any human action that damages our common home and endangers the life and survival of our common household, especially our most vulnerable brothers and sisters, becomes a sin. The various manifestations of the ecological crisis are not mere natural disasters as they are still largely seen by the general public. No ecological imbalance comes about by itself. The ecological crisis is a consequence of our own values, beliefs, and conscious choices, and ultimately of our sinful behavior.

Ecumenical Patriarch Bartholomew I is the religious leader who, more than anyone else, has spoken of ecological sin. For him, "Each human act that contributes to the destruction of the natural environment must be regarded as a very serious sin."[5]

4. John Zizioulas (Metropolitan of Pergamon), "Foreword," in *Cosmic Grace Humble Prayer: The Ecological Vision of the Green Patriarch Bartholomew*, ed. John Chryssavgis (Grand Rapids, MI: Eerdmans, 2009), viii.

5. Ecumenical Patriarch Bartholomew I, "Greeting during the Symposium at Holy Trinity Monastery, Halki, June 1, 1992," in *Cosmic Grace, Humble Prayer*, ed. John Chryssavgis (Grand Rapids, MI: Eerdmans, 2003), 84.

Accordingly, every harm to the creation of the almighty God, "even out of negligence, constitutes not simply an evil, but a grave sin."[6] Pope Francis quotes the ecumenical patriarch's views on ecological sin in the preamble to the encyclical:

> Patriarch Bartholomew has spoken in particular of the need for each of us to repent of the ways we have harmed the planet, for "inasmuch as we all generate small ecological damage," we are called to acknowledge "our contribution, smaller or greater, to the disfigurement and destruction of creation."[7] He has repeatedly stated this firmly and persuasively, challenging us to acknowledge our sins against creation. . . . For "to commit a crime against the natural world is a sin against ourselves and a sin against God."[8] (8)

In line with the integral ecology and relational metaphysics that characterizes the encyclical throughout, Pope Francis understands sin as the rupture of fundamental relationships in life. He recalls in this regard the creation accounts in the book of Genesis which conceive human life as grounded in the closely intertwined relationships with God, with one's fellow human beings, and with the whole of creation. Sin is precisely the rupture of "these three vital relationships" outwardly and within us:

> The creation accounts in the book of Genesis contain, in their own symbolic and narrative language, profound

6. Bartholomew I, "Message of the Synaxis of Hierarchs of the Ecumenical Patriarchate, September 1, 1998," in *Cosmic Grace, Humble Prayer*, ed. Chryssavgis, 201.

7. Bartholomew I, *Message for the Day of Prayer for the Protection of Creation* (1 September 2012).

8. Bartholomew I, *Address in Santa Barbara, California* (8 November 1997); cf. John Chryssavgis, *On Earth as in Heaven: Ecological Vision and Initiatives of Ecumenical Patriarch Bartholomew* (New York: Fordham University Press, 2012).

teachings about human existence and its historical reality. They suggest that human life is grounded in three funda- mental and closely intertwined relationships: with God, with our neighbour and with the earth itself. According to the Bible, these three vital relationships have been broken, both outwardly and within us. This rupture is sin. (66)

It is only within a relational view of reality, where every- thing is interrelated and interdependent, that the concept of ecological sin makes sense. Nothing in creation exists in isola- tion. There exists a physical and spiritual connectedness be- tween all of creation. Sin is precisely the distortion of this underlying and all-embracing relational unity. As the ortho- dox theologian John Chryssavgis writes, the root of human- ity's original sin is "not a transgression against some invisible 'principle,' but the rupture of the primal connection between ourselves, our world, and our God."[9]

We shall now reflect on the various layers of ecological sin as a rupture of fundamental relationships with the Creator, with our fellow human beings, and with the rest of creation.

The Triple Layers of Ecological Sin

Our devastation of our own common planetary home is a sin against God, humanity, and the world. It ruptures the bonds of divine, human, and cosmic fellowship.[10]

Ecological sin is first and above all, a sin against God, the Creator. All of creation is a message of love from God. To disregard that message, to deliberately misuse God's gifts, is sinful. It constitutes nothing less than disrespect toward the

9. John Chryssavgis, "Foreword," in *The Sermon of All Creation: Chris- tians on Nature*, ed. Judith Fitzgerald and Michael Oren Fitzgerald (Bloomington, IN: World Wisdom, 2005), vii.

10. See Kureethadam, *Creation in Crisis*, 341–45.

Creator. As Ecumenical Patriarch Bartholomew has written: "All that was created "good" by the All Good Creator participates in His sacredness. Conversely, disrespect toward nature is disrespect toward the Creator, just as the arrogant destruction of a work of art is an insult to the artist who created it."[11]

Ecological sin is the rupturing of the most important of all relationships, namely, the bond with the Creator. This truth is supremely evident in the original sin of Adam and Eve. The disobedience of Adam and Eve, while dwelling in the garden lovingly created for them, to respect a limit imposed on them regarding a tree in the same garden, shattered above all their relationship with the Creator. Adam and Eve had originally walked with God in the garden, enjoying God's friendship and the goodness of creation. With sin, there creeps in a profound alienation between God and humanity, between the creatures and the Creator. "When they heard God walking in the garden, they hid among the trees. The God whose purpose in creating was to enter into and facilitate loving relationships was rejected by the creatures chosen to bear his image."[12] As Pope Francis notes in *Laudato Si'*, "The harmony between the Creator, humanity and creation as a whole was disrupted by our presuming to take the place of God and refusing to acknowledge our creaturely limitations" (66). The ecological crisis—our refusal to accept and respect the natural order of things—is a sin against the Creator, longing to "be like God" and pretending to substitute for him.

11. Bartholomew I, "Homily at the Fiftieth Anniversary Dedication of St Barbara Greek Orthodox Church in Santa Barbara, California, November 8, 1997," in *Cosmic Grace, Humble Prayer*, ed. Chryssavgis, 214.

12. Dave Bookless, *Planet Wise: Dare to Care for God's World* (Nottingham: Inter-Varsity Press, 2008), 36.

The sin here is regarding humanity and the world as autonomous and without the need of God.

In second place, the ecological crisis is a sin against our fellow human beings. The crisis ruptures the real bonds of human fellowship. In this regard, to pollute land, water, and atmosphere and to endanger the health of fellow citizens is clearly a sin! In the case of anthropogenic climate change, excessive emissions of greenhouse gases, especially by the rich countries, which have direct consequences on poorer and vulnerable communities elsewhere, is obviously a sin! Causing climate change which can in turn exacerbate the already precarious situation of food security in the world, or endanger health security of poor communities, or cause forced mass migration, is clearly a sin!

The ecological crisis reveals, above all, how we have betrayed the eucharistic vocation of human communities, namely, to share the gifts of creation with all the members of our common household in a spirit of communion (*koinonia*), like the one bread broken and shared at the table of the Lord. The unequal distribution and consumption of our home planet's life-essential resources, and the tragic fact that nearly one in seven of our fellow humans go to bed hungry every night, is indeed a grave moral sin against the eucharistic nature of human communities. The natural environment is a collective good and to appropriate more of one's due share of it is clearly a sin. Pope Francis writes in *Laudato Si'*, citing an appropriate passage from a statement from the Catholic Bishops' Conference of New Zealand:

> The natural environment is a collective good, the patrimony of all humanity and the responsibility of everyone. If we make something our own, it is only to administer it for the good of all. If we do not, we burden our consciences with the weight of having denied the existence of others. That is why the New Zealand bishops asked what the commandment

"Thou shalt not kill" means when "twenty percent of the world's population consumes resources at a rate that robs the poor nations and future generations of what they need to survive."[13] (95)

The contemporary ecological crisis reveals how we are also sinning against future generations by leaving them a home with polluted land, water, and atmosphere, a planet scarce in resources as we already consume the renewable natural resources at a totally unsustainable rate, and a climate that is fast turning awry. As Pope Francis reminds us, "The notion of the common good also extends to future generations" (159). He also asks "that those who are obsessed with maximizing profits will stop to reflect on the environmental damage which they will leave behind for future generations?" (190).

Third, the ecological sin is, from a theological perspective, an offence against creation itself. When humans devastate our home planet, it is sin, in as much as it constitutes a disobedience to the divine command to care for the rest of creation, to "guard" and "cultivate" the terrestrial garden (see Gen 2:15). In *Laudato Si'*, Pope Francis recalls the incisive teaching of Ecumenical Patriarch Bartholomew in this regard: "For human beings . . . to destroy the biological diversity of God's creation; for human beings to degrade the integrity of the earth by causing changes in its climate, by stripping the earth of its natural forests or destroying its wetlands; for human beings to contaminate the earth's waters, its land, its air, and its life—these are sins"[14] (8).

The pope reminds us that we have an obligation to respect the laws of nature and the relationships that exist among creatures:

13. New Zealand Catholic Bishops Conference, *Statement on Environmental Issues* (1 September 2006).

14. *Address in Santa Barbara, California* (8 November 1997); cf. Chryssavgis, *On Earth as in Heaven*.

This responsibility for God's earth means that human beings, endowed with intelligence, must respect the laws of
nature and the delicate equilibria existing between the
creatures of this world, for "he commanded and they were
created; and he established them for ever and ever; he fixed
their bounds and he set a law which cannot pass away"
(*Ps* 148:5b-6). The laws found in the Bible dwell on relationships, not only among individuals but also with other living beings. "You shall not see your brother's donkey or his
ox fallen down by the way and withhold your help. . . .
If you chance to come upon a bird's nest in any tree or on
the ground, with young ones or eggs and the mother sitting
upon the young or upon the eggs; you shall not take the
mother with the young" (*Dt* 22:4, 6). Along these same
lines, rest on the seventh day is meant not only for human
beings, but also so "that your ox and your donkey may
have rest" (*Ex* 23:12). (68)

The multiple manifestations of the ecological crisis—from
pollution and profligate consumption to biodiversity loss and
climate change—are all expressions of humanity's sinful con-
duct toward God's creation.

Repercussions of Human Sin on the Natural World

From a theological point of view, there exists a significant
link between human sin and the state of the physical world.[15]
Sin literally defiles the land. In the faith traditions of humanity, and in the biblical tradition in particular, the land acts as
a spiritual barometer of the moral lives of its inhabitants.

In *Laudato Si'*, Pope Francis notes that the rupture of humanity's relationship with God "distorted our mandate to
'have dominion' over the earth (cf. *Gen* 1:28), to 'till it and

---

15. See Kureethadam, *Creation in Crisis*, 351–58.

keep it' (*Gen* 2:15). As a result, the originally harmonious relationship between human beings and nature became con-flictual (cf. *Gen* 3:17-19)" (66). We may recall in this regard what Pope John Paul II and Ecumenical Patriarch Bar-tholomew I wrote in their common declaration in 2002: "At the beginning of history, man and woman sinned by disobey-ing God and rejecting His design for creation. Among the results of this first sin was the destruction of the original harmony of creation."[16] The disharmony created by original sin casts a gloomy shadow over the whole of creation. Pope John Paul II wrote in the 1990 Message:

> Made in the image and likeness of god, Adam and Eve were to have exercised their dominion over the earth (*Gen* 1:28) with wisdom and love. Instead, they destroyed the existing harmony by deliberately going against the Creator's plan, that is, by choosing to sin. This resulted not only in man's alienation from himself, in death and fratricide, but also in the earth's 'rebellion' against him (cf. *Gen* 3:17-19; 4:12).[17]

Pope Francis reminds us in *Laudato Si'* that sin against one's own fellow humans can have negative repercussions for the land and for creation as a whole. Fratricide can lead to ecocide as it is tragically exemplified in the story of Cain and Abel in the fourth chapter of the book of Genesis, of which Pope Francis offers an ecological interpretation:

> In the story of Cain and Abel, we see how envy led Cain to commit the ultimate injustice against his brother, which

16. Pope John Paul II and Ecumenical Patriarch Bartholomew I, "Common Declaration on the Environment" (June 10, 2002).

17. John Paul II, *Peace with God the Creator, Peace with All of Creation*, n. 3.

in turn ruptured the relationship between Cain and God, and between Cain and the earth from which he was banished. This is seen clearly in the dramatic exchange between God and Cain. God asks: "Where is Abel your brother?" Cain answers that he does not know, and God persists: "What have you done? The voice of your brother's blood is crying to me from the ground. And now you are cursed from the ground" (*Gen* 4:9-11). Disregard for the duty to cultivate and maintain a proper relationship with my neighbour, for whose care and custody I am responsible, ruins my relationship with my own self, with others, with God and with the earth. (70)

As in every sin, Cain's anger against his brother is also a revolt against God. Cain refuses to accept both God's supremacy and coexistence with his own brother. Just as Adam refused to *keep* the garden through his disobedience, Cain refuses to be a *keeper* of his own brother. He refuses any positive relationship by watching, protecting, taking care of his younger brother. In fact "the Hebrew word for *keeping* used here is exactly the same that originally had described Adam's task with regard to the garden: taking care, preserving next to serving."[18] The fratricide has direct repercussions on the land as we read in the verses that immediately follow. The field, the ground, exactly where bushes and plants were to grow (Gen 2:5), the garden entrusted to humanity to "till it and keep it" (Gen 2:15) is now soaked with the innocent blood of Abel that cries out to the Creator. As a consequence of sin, the land becomes barren. The very land out of which "God made to grow every tree that is pleasant to the sight and good for food" (Gen 2:9), basking in God's original blessing of

18. Brigitte Kahl, "Fratricide and Ecocide: Rereading Genesis 2–4," in *Earth Habitat: Eco-Injustice and the Church's Response*, ed. Dieter Hessel and Larry Rasmussen (Minneapolis: Fortress Press, 2001), 62.

creation, is now cursed along with the sinner and loses its natural fertility.

The Bible contains several instances of the impact of human sin on creation, often with graphic descriptions of the devastation of the land. The sins of humanity, especially in the form of social injustice, have direct and dire consequences on all other forms of life. Pope Francis reiterates this truth in the context of the biblical narration of Noah and the Great Flood:

> When all these relationships are neglected, when justice no longer dwells in the land, the Bible tells us that life itself is endangered. We see this in the story of Noah, where God threatens to do away with humanity because of its constant failure to fulfil the requirements of justice and peace: "I have determined to make an end of all flesh; for the earth is filled with violence through them" (*Gen* 6:13). These ancient stories, full of symbolism, bear witness to a conviction which we today share, that everything is interconnected, and that genuine care for our own lives and our relationships with nature is inseparable from fraternity, justice and faithfulness to others. (70)

According to Pope Francis, the Noah story is indeed paradigmatic of how the defilement of creation through human sin has repercussions also on the rest of creation, with even innocent animals caught up in the punishment inflicted on guilty humans. The death-dealing curse on land and on living things closely follow human sin—just as shadows follow light—as evident in the Great Flood which led to the obliteration of all life on Earth, except for Noah and his family, and the creatures that found shelter in his ark. As sin multiplied on Earth, the very waters in which according to God's original project living creatures were called to swarm and multiply (Gen 1:20-22) ended up kissing them with death. "And all flesh died that moved on the earth, birds, domestic animals, wild animals, all swarming creatures that swarm on the earth, and all human beings; everything on dry land in whose nostrils was the breath of life died" (Gen 7:21-22).

The contemporary ecological crisis, which is markedly anthropogenic (human induced) in character, reveals how human sin has concrete repercussions on the rest of creation. Ecological problems are ultimately sin problems. What we are seeing in the world today is ample evidence of this truth. "We cannot disobey with impunity. There are limits to how far we can push our rebellion against God when it comes to his creation. After too much abuse, the land will refuse to produce crops. The ocean will stop yielding fish. Wells will dry up. Rules matter. Sin has consequences."[19] As Pope Francis points out in the encyclical, "environmental deterioration and human and ethical degradation are closely linked" (56).

"The wages of sin is death," wrote St. Paul in the letter to the Romans (Rom 6:23). This truth is clearly evident in the contemporary ecological crisis. Our continued sin, our persistent sinful behavior, is preventing the healing of the land. It is time for us to repent and reconcile ourselves with the Creator and the rest of creation once again.

Response to Ecological Sin: Repentance and Reconciliation

The only valid response to ecological sin—our rupturing of the bonds of fellowship with the Creator, with our fellow human beings, and with the rest of creation—is repentance and reconciliation. In *Laudato Si'*, Pope Francis cites Ecumenical Patriarch Bartholomew on the need for repentance:

---

19. Edward Brown, *Our Father's World: Mobilizing the Church to Care for Creation* (South Hadley, MA: Doorlight Publications, 2006), 59.

"Patriarch Bartholomew has spoken in particular of the need for each of us to repent of the ways we have harmed the planet, for 'inasmuch as we all generate small ecological damage,' we are called to acknowledge 'our contribution, smaller or greater, to the disfigurement and destruction of creation' "[20] (8).

Since the root cause of the contemporary ecological crisis is human sin and human selfishness, what we need, in the very first place, is deep repentance or *metanoia*. We may cite Ecumenical Patriarch Bartholomew I in this regard:

> The root cause of our environmental sin lies in our self-centredness and in the mistaken order of values that we inherit and accept without any critical evaluation. We need a new way of thinking about our own selves, about our relationship with the world and with God. Without this revolutionary "change of mind," all our conservation projects, however well intentioned, will remain ultimately ineffective. For we shall be dealing only with the symptoms, not with their cause. Lectures and international conferences may help to awaken our conscience, but what is truly required is a baptism of tears.[21]

In *Laudato Si'*, Pope Francis speaks of reconciliation with the rest of creation, a sort of universal reconciliation that needs to follow our repentance for our sins against creation. If ecological sin is a rupture of fundamental human relationships with the Creator and the rest of creation, what we need

20. Bartholomew I, *Message for the Day of Prayer for the Protection of Creation* (1 September 2012).

21. Bartholomew I, "Closing Address during the Concluding Ceremony for the Fourth International and Interreligious Symposium on the Adriatic Sea, June 10, 2002," in *Cosmic Grace, Humble Prayer*, ed. Chryssavgis, 276.

today is precisely to heal such a rupture. "It is significant that the harmony which Saint Francis of Assisi experienced with all creatures was seen as a healing of that rupture" (66). This healing can lead to true reconciliation and even to recovery of our original innocence and harmony with the rest of creation. He proposes St. Francis of Assisi as a model on this path: "Saint Bonaventure held that, through universal reconciliation with every creature, Saint Francis in some way returned to the state of original innocence"[22] (66).

Our true repentance for the precarious state of our common home can be measured to the extent that each of us own up to our responsibility for the harm we are causing to the planetary nest that shelters us. As the biblical scholar Nicholas King points out, "It is a profoundly biblical instinct to recognize that I am part of the problem, as, for example, David is forced to do in 2 Samuel 11 and 12, after his adultery with Bathsheba and the murder of her husband."[23] In *Laudato Si'*, Pope Francis invites each of us to see the truth of our responsibility for the state of the planet, "challenging us to acknowledge our sins against creation" (8). Such a deep and personal repentance alone can lead to ecological conversion with which we shall be dealing in the third part of our commentary in the context of responding to the crisis of our common home.

22. Cf. Bonaventure, *The Major Legend of Saint Francis*, VIII, 1, in *Francis of Assisi: Early Documents*, vol. 2 (New York: New City Press, 2000), 586.

23. Nicholas King, "*Laudato Si'*: A Biblical Angle," *The Way* 54 (2015), 28.

Acknowledge the Human Roots of the Crisis of Our Common Home

In *Laudato Si'*, Pope Francis offers a profound analysis of humanity's earthly predicament.[1] A fundamental moment in the process of judging the crisis of our common home is the search for its underlying deeper causes. As Pope Francis says at the beginning of the third chapter of the encyclical, "It would hardly be helpful to describe the symptoms without acknowledging the human origins of the ecological crisis" (101). In fact, assuming responsibility for a problem we have caused is the very first step in solving the same problem. In this regard, Pope Francis invites us in the encyclical to own up to our responsibility for the precarious state of our common home. He dedicates an entire chapter to "The Human Roots of the Ecological Crisis." He wants to offer a deeper "diagnosis" of the underlying roots of the malaise, before going on to elaborate lines of action, policy recommendations, and spiritual exhortations later in the encyclical.

1. Mike Hulme, "Finding the Message of the Pope's Encyclical," *Environment: Science and Policy for Sustainable Development* 57/6 (2015), 16.

Our fifth green commandment is about the deeper human roots of the degradation of our common home as presented in *Laudato Si'*. We begin with a reflection on the anthropogenic character of the contemporary ecological crisis, that is, the realization that the crisis is caused by human activities. We will then go on to trace the human roots of the ecological crisis in the overarching technocratic paradigm, which, according to Pope Francis, seeks to dominate and exploit the natural world. However, as the pope notes with great intuition, behind such a paradigm lurk the deeper conceptual root causes of the ecological crisis. Following Pope Francis's lead, we will identity two of them: modern anthropocentrism that has led to humanity's oppressive lordship over the natural world and a mechanistic conception of nature as inert matter, a storehouse of resources, which is also a key underlying assumption of modern economy. We will conclude with a reflection on the need for a radical cultural and conceptual paradigm shift on the part of humanity in order to care for our common home.

The "Human" Roots of the Crisis

What stands out about the contemporary ecological crisis is its conspicuously anthropogenic character. The word *anthropogenic* is increasingly used in scientific parlance to emphasize that the precarious state of our common home is caused by humans themselves. It is precisely the anthropogenic origin of the ecological crisis which motivates the search for the deeper causes of the malaise, as Pope Francis attempts to do in *Laudato Si'*.

Paradoxically, the anthropogenic character of the contemporary ecological crisis, namely, that it is caused by human activities, continues to be denied by some people, despite overwhelming scientific evidence to the contrary. It is particularly evident in the case of the so-called sceptics of human-induced climate change. There are others who do not deny the crisis of our common home but remain largely indifferent to it. Pope Francis considers both of these positions as grossly irresponsible. "Obstructionist attitudes, even on the part of believers, can range from denial of the problem to indifference, nonchalant resignation or blind confidence in technical solutions" (14). The irresponsible attitudes of denial and indifference are indeed self-destructive in times of crisis.

In *Laudato Si'*, Pope Francis takes pains to acknowledge that the various manifestations of the contemporary ecological crisis are indeed caused by humans. With regard to climate change, for example, he writes: "A number of scientific studies indicate that most global warming in recent decades is due to the great concentration of greenhouse gases (carbon dioxide, methane, nitrogen oxides and others) released mainly as a result of human activity" (23). Pope Francis has solid scientific backing in this regard. Today there is nearly unanimous consensus in the scientific community about the anthropogenic effect on climate change.[2] Human responsibility for the current ecological crisis is equally evident when it comes to the problem of the mass extinction of species. Pope Francis reechos the scientific consensus about human-induced biodiversity loss: "Each year sees the disappearance of thousands of plant and animal species. . . . The great majority become extinct for reasons related to human activity" (33).

2. See John Cook et al., "Quantifying the Consensus on Anthropogenic Global Warming in the Scientific Literature," *Environmental Research Letters* 8 (2013), 024024; Naomi Oreskes, "Beyond the Ivory Tower: The Scientific Consensus on Climate Change," *Science* 306 (2004), 1686; National Academy of Sciences Committee on the Science of Climate Change, *Climate Change Science: An Analysis of Some Key Questions* (Washington, DC: National Academy Press, 2001), 3.

Human-induced changes to the earth's climate, land, oceans, and biosphere are now significant and so rapid that it may be time to speak of a new geological epoch defined by the action of humans.[3] The dramatic transformation of the home planet on account of human activities in recent times has led many scientists to claim that the home planet is now being forcefully ushered into a new geological epoch altogether. The term proposed to evidence this quantitative shift in the relationship between humans and the rest of the natural world is *Anthropocene*,[4] namely, *the age of the humans*. It was proposed by Nobel Laureate Paul J. Crutzen—a prominent and long-standing member of the Pontifical Academy of Sciences which advices the pope on scientific matters—more than a decade ago.[5] Today, as the 2012 *Planet Under Pressure Conference* noted, "Humans have become a prime driver of change at the planetary level, significantly altering earth's biological, chemical and physical processes."[6]

3. Jan Zalasiewicz et al., "The Anthropocene: A New Epoch of Geological Time?," *Philosophical Transactions of the Royal Society A* 369 (2011), 835–41.

4. The word combines the root "anthropo," meaning "human" with the "-cene," the standard suffix for "epoch" in geologic time. The Anthropocene is distinguished as a new period either after or within the Holocene, the current epoch, which began approximately 10,000 years ago (about 8000 BCE) with the end of the last glacial period.

5. See P. J. Crutzen and E. F. Stoermer, "The Anthropocene," *Global Change Newsletter* 41 (2000), 17–18; Crutzen, "Geology of Mankind: the Anthropocene," *Nature* 415 (2002), 23. On the antecedents of the anthropocene concept, see Will Steffen et al., "The Anthropocene: Conceptual and Historical Perspectives," *Philosophical Transactions of the Royal Society A* 369 (2011), 843–45.

6. International Conference Planet Under Pressure, *Rio+20 Policy Brief* (London, 26–29 March 2012), 1.

As Lynn White noted already in 1967 in his epoch-making article: "Surely no creature other than man has ever managed to foul its nest in such short order."[7]

We humans are pulling down the very pillars of our common planetary home, as is evident in the anthropogenic character of the contemporary ecological crisis. Why are we fouling the very nest that shelters us? Here we need to discover the deeper underlying roots of the contemporary ecological crisis, as Pope Francis tells us in *Laudato Si'*. It is to this task that we turn now.

The Roots of the Ecological Crisis in the Dominant Technocratic Paradigm

What is original about *Laudato Si'* is that the encyclical attempts an analysis of the deeper human roots of the deterioration of our common home. Pope Francis announces already in the introduction that he will "attempt to get to *the roots* of the present situation, so as to consider not only its symptoms but also its *deeper causes*" (15; italics added).

The underlying deeper human roots of the crisis of our common home are multiple, given the very complexity of the ecological crisis (63). However, Pope Francis is quick to note that they have ultimately to do with a mind-set, a worldview, a particular way of perceiving the natural world and relating with it. He calls it the "dominant technocratic paradigm":

A certain way of understanding human life and activity has gone awry, to the serious detriment of the world around us. Should we not pause and consider this? At this

7. Lynn White, "The Historic Roots of Our Ecologic Crisis," *Science* 155 (1967), 1204.

stage, I propose that we focus on the dominant technocratic paradigm and the place of human beings and of human action in the world. (101)

According to Pope Francis, "Humanity has entered a new era in which our technical prowess has brought us to a crossroads" (102). "Technoscience," the pope notes, "can produce important means of improving the quality of human life, from useful domestic appliances to great transportation systems, bridges, buildings and public spaces" (103). "It is right to rejoice in these advances and to be excited by the immense possibilities which they continue to open up before us" (102). Citing Pope John Paul II, Pope Francis reminds us that "science and technology are wonderful products of a God-given human creativity."[8] The pope comments that "the modification of nature for useful purposes has distinguished the human family from the beginning" and points out, citing Pope Benedict XVI, that technology itself "expresses the inner tension that impels man gradually to overcome material limitations"[9] (102).

Pope Francis is aware that technology has given us "an impressive dominance over the whole of humanity and the entire world" (104). He is concerned precisely about the unlimited and unprecedented power that technology has placed in human hands and cites occasions in the past when it has been abused:

Yet it must also be recognized that nuclear energy, biotechnology, information technology, knowledge of our DNA,

8. Pope John Paul II, *Address to Scientists and Representatives of the United Nations University*, Hiroshima (25 February 1981), 3: *AAS* 73 (1981), 422.

9. Pope Benedict XVI, Encyclical Letter *Caritas in Veritate* (29 June 2009), 69: *AAS* 101 (2009), 702.

and many other abilities which we have acquired, have given us tremendous power. . . . Never has humanity had such power over itself, yet nothing ensures that it will be used wisely, particularly when we consider how it is currently being used. We need but think of the nuclear bombs dropped in the middle of the twentieth century, or the array of technology which Nazism, Communism and other totalitarian regimes have employed to kill millions of people, to say nothing of the increasingly deadly arsenal of weapons available for modern warfare. In whose hands does all this power lie, or will it eventually end up? It is extremely risky for a small part of humanity to have it. (104)

Pope Francis proceeds to offer some very critical observations of modern technology, in the footsteps of Romano Guardini, one of his favorite intellectual masters. The pope is critical of the "tendency to believe that every increase in power means 'an increase of "progress" itself,' an advance in 'security, usefulness, welfare and vigour; . . . an assimilation of new values into the stream of culture,'[10] as if reality, goodness and truth automatically flow from technological and economic power as such." The pope concurs with Guardini's observation that "contemporary man has not been trained to use power well."[11] According to the pope, it is so "because our immense technological development has not been accompanied by a development in human responsibility, values and conscience, and 'power is never considered in terms of the responsibility of choice which is inherent in freedom' "[12] (105).

---

10. Romano Guardini, *Das Ende der Neuzeit*, 9th ed. (Würzburg, 1965), 87 (English: *The End of the Modern World* [Wilmington, 1998], 82).

11. Ibid.

12. Ibid., 87–88 (*The End of the Modern World*, 83).

The problem is the globalization of the technocratic paradigm which has become entirely dominant in human affairs.
Technology now controls and "lords over" both human beings and the natural world. The pope writes, drawing inspiration once again from Guardini:

> The technological paradigm has become so dominant that
> it would be difficult to do without its resources and even
> more difficult to utilize them without being dominated by
> their internal logic. It has become countercultural to choose
> a lifestyle whose goals are even partly independent of tech-
> nology, of its costs and its power to globalize and make us
> all the same. Technology tends to absorb everything into
> its ironclad logic, and those who are surrounded with tech-
> nology "know full well that it moves forward in the final
> analysis neither for profit nor for the well-being of the
> human race," that "in the most radical sense of the term
> power is its motive—a lordship over all."[13] As a result,
> "man seizes hold of the naked elements of both nature and
> human nature."[14] Our capacity for making decisions, a
> more genuine freedom and the space for each one's alterna-
> tive creativity are diminished. (108)

Pope Francis notes in the encyclical how the modern technocratic paradigm tends to dominate various spheres of
human life: social, economic, ethical, and so forth. On the
social level, "many problems of today's world stem from the
tendency, at times unconscious, to make the method and aims
of science and technology an epistemological paradigm
which shapes the lives of individuals and the workings of
society. . . . Technological products are not neutral, for they
create a framework which ends up conditioning lifestyles

13. Ibid., 63–64 (*The End of the Modern World,* 56).
14. Ibid., 64 (*The End of the Modern World,* 56).

and shaping social possibilities along the lines dictated by the interests of certain powerful groups." The technocratic paradigm ends up determining "the kind of society we want to build" (107). The technocratic paradigm extends its tentacles to the economic spheres as well. "The economy accepts every advance in technology with a view to profit, without concern for its potentially negative impact on human beings. Finance overwhelms the real economy." Accordingly, "we have 'a sort of "superdevelopment" of a wasteful and consumerist kind which forms an unacceptable contrast with the ongoing situations of dehumanizing deprivation,'[15] while we are all too slow in developing economic institutions and social initiatives which can give the poor regular access to basic resources" (109). Pope Francis notes with sadness that we live in a world deprived of "genuine ethical horizons to which one can appeal. Life gradually becomes a surrender to situations conditioned by technology, itself viewed as the principal key to the meaning of existence" (110).

The dominant technocratic paradigm is thus clearly in the docks for the crisis of our planetary home and of our common human family. However, Pope Francis goes a step further and searches for the deeper conceptual roots behind the very technocratic paradigm: "We fail to see the deepest roots of our present failures, which have to do with the direction, goals, meaning and social implications of technological and economic growth" (109). What are the "deepest roots" of the dominant technocratic paradigm which holds in its "ironclad logic" (108) our mode of living and operating in the world today? It is to these that we turn our attention now.

15. Benedict XVI, *Caritas in Veritate*, 22: *AAS*, 657.

Deeper Roots of the Crisis: Modern Anthropocentrism and the Mechanistic Vision of the Natural World

According to Pope Francis, to get to the deeper human roots of the contemporary ecological crisis, we need to get to the underlying conceptual foundations of the reigning dominant technocratic paradigm. As he notes, "The basic problem goes even deeper: it is the way that humanity has taken up technology and its development *according to an undifferentiated and one-dimensional paradigm*" (106). The basic constituents of such a conceptual paradigm are the exalted position of the subject as in modern anthropocentrism, the reduction of the world to a mere object as in the mechanistic conception of the natural world as inert matter for human use and consumption, and consequently, a conflictual relationship between humanity and the natural world. Significantly, all these elements are present in the following dense paragraph from *Laudato Si'*:

> This paradigm exalts the concept of a subject who, using logical and rational procedures, progressively approaches and gains control over an external object. This subject makes every effort to establish the scientific and experimental method, which in itself is already a technique of possession, mastery and transformation. It is as if the subject were to find itself in the presence of something formless, completely open to manipulation. Men and women have constantly intervened in nature, but for a long time this meant being in tune with and respecting the possibilities offered by the things themselves. It was a matter of receiving what nature itself allowed, as if from its own hand. Now, by contrast, we are the ones to lay our hands on things, attempting to extract everything possible from them while frequently ignoring or forgetting the reality in front of us. Human beings and material objects no longer extend a friendly hand to one another; the relationship has become confrontational. (106)

In *Laudato Si'*, Pope Francis is particularly critical of anthropocentrism. He notes how "modernity has been marked by an excessive anthropocentrism" (116). According to him, "Men and women of our postmodern world run the risk of rampant individualism, and many problems of society are connected with today's self-centred culture of instant gratification" (162). In the pope's view, the disastrous state of our common home has to do with the tendency on the part of humanity to make itself the absolute center of reality. The abuse of creation begins when human beings arbitrarily posit themselves at the center. Citing Pope Benedict XVI, Pope Francis writes that "creation is harmed 'where we ourselves have the final word, where everything is simply our property and we use it for ourselves alone. The misuse of creation begins when we no longer recognize any higher instance than ourselves, when we see nothing else but ourselves' "[16] (6). The ecological crisis is itself a sort of rebellion from the part of nature to humanity's tyrannical lordship over it:

> Once the human being declares independence from reality and behaves with absolute dominion, the very foundations of our life begin to crumble, for "instead of carrying out his role as a cooperator with God in the work of creation, man sets himself up in place of God and thus ends up provoking a rebellion on the part of nature."[17] (117)

Within an anthropocentric perspective, human relationship with nature tends to become despotic and exploitative, since the latter is perceived exclusively in terms of human interests. In modern anthropocentrism, the physical world is seen to

16. Benedict XVI, *Address to the Clergy of the Diocese of Bolzano-Bressanone* (6 August 2008): *AAS* 100 (2008), 634.
17. John Paul II, Encyclical Letter *Centesimus Annus* (1 May 1991), 37: *AAS* 83 (1991), 840.

exist at the disposal of humans and as incapable of posing any limit whatsoever to the human quest for conquest and mastery. A line of thought oriented toward possession and domination of nature inevitably leads to a voracious and exploitative attitude toward it. In this regard, Pope Francis notes that "we have come to see ourselves as her lords and masters, entitled to plunder her at will" (2).

According to Pope Francis, "A misguided anthropocentrism leads to a misguided lifestyle. . . . When human beings place themselves at the centre, they give absolute priority to immediate convenience and all else becomes relative." Relativism "sees everything as irrelevant unless it serves one's own immediate interests" (122). The pope goes on to add that such a self-centered relativism inevitably leads not only to environmental degradation but also to social decay:

> The culture of relativism is the same disorder which drives one person to take advantage of another, to treat others as mere objects, imposing forced labour on them or enslaving them to pay their debts. The same kind of thinking leads to the sexual exploitation of children and abandonment of the elderly who no longer serve our interests. . . . Is it not the same relativistic logic which justifies buying the organs of the poor for resale or use in experimentation, or eliminating children because they are not what their parents wanted? This same "use and throw away" logic generates so much waste, because of the disordered desire to consume more than what is really necessary. We should not think that political efforts or the force of law will be sufficient to prevent actions which affect the environment because, when the culture itself is corrupt and objective truth and universally valid principles are no longer upheld, then laws can only be seen as arbitrary impositions or obstacles to be avoided. (123)

Modern anthropocentrism which exalts the individual over everything else, the pope notes, also "continues to stand in the way of shared understanding and of any effort to strengthen social bonds." Modern anthropocentrism is ultimately based on a false anthropology and a distorted view of the relationship between humanity and the natural world: "An inadequate presentation of Christian anthropology gave rise to a wrong understanding of the relationship between human beings and the world," namely, "a Promethean vision of mastery over the world." Instead, the pope reminds us that "our 'dominion' over the universe should be understood more properly in the sense of responsible stewardship"[18] (116). "Clearly, the Bible has no place for a tyrannical anthropocentrism unconcerned for other creatures" (68).

In *Laudato Si'*, Pope Francis warns that modern anthropocentrism is detrimental ultimately to humans themselves:

> When human beings fail to find their true place in this world, they misunderstand themselves and end up acting against themselves: "Not only has God given the earth to man, who must use it with respect for the original good purpose for which it was given, but, man too is God's gift to man. He must therefore respect the natural and moral structure with which he has been endowed."[19] (115)

An authentic ecology stands in need of an "adequate anthropology" (118). The reaction to excessive anthropocentrism cannot be biocentrism as it has been done in certain schools of environmental philosophy like deep ecology. Biocentrism swings the pendulum to the other extreme by placing the natural world at the center and denying human uniqueness altogether. The pope writes in this regard:

18. Cf. *Love for Creation: An Asian Response to the Ecological Crisis*, Declaration of the Colloquium sponsored by the Federation of Asian Bishops' Conferences (Tagatay, 31 January–5 February 1993), 3.3.2.

19. John Paul II, *Centesimus Annus*, 38: *AAS*, 841.

> There can be no renewal of our relationship with nature
> without a renewal of humanity itself. . . . When the
> human person is considered as simply one being among
> others, the product of chance or physical determinism, then
> "our overall sense of responsibility wanes."[20] A misguided
> anthropocentrism need not necessarily yield to "biocen-
> trism," for that would entail adding yet another imbalance,
> failing to solve present problems and adding new ones.
> Human beings cannot be expected to feel responsibility for
> the world unless, at the same time, their unique capacities
> of knowledge, will, freedom and responsibility are recog-
> nized and valued. (118)

Modern anthropocentrism is dialectically linked to the
modern mechanistic vision of the natural world. Anthropocentrism, in exalting the human subject to a position of absolute centrality, has led to the depreciation and abuse of the
surrounding natural world. Once the subject becomes the
Archimedean center as in modern anthropocentrism, the rest
of physical reality comes to be seen as nothing but a gigantic
reservoir of objects or raw materials destined for human consumption. Pope Francis quotes Pope John Paul II, who wrote
in his first encyclical that human beings frequently seem "to
see no other meaning in their natural environment than what
serves for immediate use and consumption"[21] (5).

Modern technological rationality, as Pope Francis points
out, citing Romano Guardini, "sees nature as an insensate
order, as a cold body of facts, as a mere 'given,' as an object of
utility, as raw material to be hammered into useful shape; it
views the cosmos similarly as a mere 'space' into which objects

20. Benedict XVI, *Message for the 2010 World Day of Peace*, 2: *AAS* 102
(2010), 41.

21. John Paul II, Encyclical Letter *Redemptor Hominis* (4 March 1979),
15: *AAS* 71 (1979), 287.

can be thrown with complete indifference"[22] (115). Within the modern mechanistic worldview, entities come to be considered as mere resources for human use and consumption with their ontological value measured only in terms of utility.

The modern mechanistic view of the natural world as a mere storehouse of resources is also largely at the basis of modern and neoliberal economies. As the pope notes, in modern economy, "nature is viewed solely as a source of profit and gain, this has serious consequences for society" (82). Pope Francis singles out for criticism "the idea of infinite or unlimited growth, which proves so attractive to economists, financiers and experts in technology" but is detrimental for our common home. The concept of unlimited growth "is based on the lie that there is an infinite supply of the earth's goods, and this leads to the planet being squeezed dry beyond every limit. It is the false notion that 'an infinite quantity of energy and resources are available, that it is possible to renew them quickly, and that the negative effects of the exploitation of the natural order can be easily absorbed' "[23] (106).

A Bold Cultural Revolution toward a New Humanism

In *Laudato Si'*, Pope Francis invites us to "broaden our vision" beyond the limited horizons of the modern technocratic paradigm. He reminds us that "we have the freedom needed to limit and direct technology; we can put it at the service of another type of progress, one which is healthier, more human, more social, more integral" (112).

22. Guardini, *Das Ende der Neuzeit*, 63 (*The End of the Modern World*, 55).

23. Pontifical Council for Justice and Peace, *Compendium of the Social Doctrine of the Church*, 462.

Pope Francis points out that today, there is "the urgent need for us to move forward in a bold cultural revolution" (114). According to the pope, such a cultural revolution toward creating a new humanity is already taking place, in spite of the continuing dominance of the current technocratic paradigm. "An authentic humanity, calling for a new synthesis, seems to dwell in the midst of our technological culture, almost unnoticed, like a mist seeping gently beneath a closed door" (112). If the ultimate roots of the degradation of our common home are ultimately human, the re-creation of harmony with the natural world can be realized only through a new humanism. "There can be no renewal of our relationship with nature without a renewal of humanity itself" (118). We need to heal fundamental human relationships. As Pope Francis indicates, "If the present ecological crisis is one small sign of the ethical, cultural and spiritual crisis of modernity, we cannot presume to heal our relationship with nature and the environment without healing all fundamental human relationships" (119).

Today, we need to heal our relationships with the natural world, with our fellow human beings, and with the Creator. A holistic and integral perspective is vital in this regard. The pope writes, "A correct relationship with the created world demands that we not weaken this social dimension of openness to others, much less the transcendent dimension of our openness to the 'Thou' of God. Our relationship with the environment can never be isolated from our relationship with others and with God" (119).

What we need today is nothing short of an integral ecology. Significantly, Pope Francis dedicates an entire chapter to it in *Laudato Si'*. We shall reflect on the concept of integral ecology in the next green commandment.

PART THREE: ACTING
(Responding to the Crisis of Our Common Home)

GREEN COMMANDMENT VI
Develop an Integral Ecology

GREEN COMMANDMENT VII
Learn a New Way of Dwelling
in Our Common Home

GREEN COMMANDMENT VIII
Educate toward Ecological Citizenship

GREEN COMMANDMENT IX
Embrace an Ecological Spirituality

GREEN COMMANDMENT X
Cultivate Ecological Virtues

Moving on with the see-judge-act methodology in our reading of Laudato Si', we have reached the third phase now. It is precisely the moment of responding to the crisis of our common home which we have sought to understand and judge in the previous two stages. It is the time to act in response to the crisis to which we dedicate the last five green commandments. We will base our reflections here mainly on the last three chapters of the encyclical.

Pope Francis argues in the encyclical that we stand in need of an integral ecology and dedicates an entire chapter to it. Many commentators have retained the concept of integral ecology as one of the most original contributions of the encyclical. The sixth green commandment is about developing an integral ecology. We will begin by indicating the underlying metaphysical vision behind the integral ecology, namely, the interrelatedness of the whole of reality and the interdependence of all created entities. The integral approach makes possible a holistic understanding of the contemporary ecological crisis and a comprehensive response to it. We will then present the two essential and constitutive elements of integral ecology as indicated by the pope, namely, its "human and social dimensions." We will conclude with a note on Saint Francis of Assisi as the model of integral ecology.

Our seventh green commandment will highlight the emphasis placed by Pope Francis in the encyclical on a new way of dwelling in our common home and managing it more responsibly. We will reflect here especially on the importance of acting together in this regard, given the magnitude and global character of the crisis. We will then point out, following what Pope Francis does in the fifth chapter of the encyclical, various levels at which we need to act: internationally, nationally, and locally. In order to care for our common home, we will need to abandon the myth of infinite growth and develop an ecological economics, respectful of the ecosystems and natural cycles of the planetary home where we dwell. We will also need a new political culture, not subservient to vested economic interests, but really at the service of the common good.

Ecological education, which is so vital for learning to care responsibly for our common home, will be the focus of our eighth green commandment. In the face of the contemporary ecological crisis, we stand in need of a deep personal transformation and a radical renewal of our lifestyles. Here the role of education is paramount. In the encyclical, Pope Francis calls for ecological education capable of establishing a new covenant between humanity and the natural world. According to the pope, we need a holistic education that can reestablish harmony with nature, our fellow human beings and the Transcendent. The pope also speaks of the variety of settings for education to ecological citizenship: schools, families, media, catechesis, houses of religious formation.

The ninth green commandment traces the contours of an ecological spirituality for our times. Creation spirituality calls for an "ecological conversion" on the part of humanity. Such a spirituality is deeply incarnational as it finds expression in concrete attitudes and gestures of care and concern for our common home and the members of our common household. It also offers a sacramental vision of the natural world as permeated by divine presence. As Pope Francis points out in the encyclical, the whole of creation bears the trinitarian imprint, as it is ultimately God's handiwork, created and constantly sustained by God's infinite love. It is also important to recall that creation's ultimate destiny is to be recapitulated in Christ in the fullness of time.

The last of our green commandments concerns the ecological virtues that we need to cultivate in order to become creative and responsible stewards of our common home. According to Pope Francis, the formation of healthy habitus for the stewardship of our common home can come only through the cultivation of appropriate "ecological virtues." Ecological virtues can lead to *a radical transformation of our lives at personal and communitarian levels. We will dwell on seven ecological virtues needed for the stewardship of our common home: praise, gratitude, care, justice, work, sobriety, and humility.*

GREEN COMMANDMENT VI
Develop an Integral Ecology

The most remarkable feature about *Laudato Si'* is its integral approach. It is not mere environmentalism or fashionable green thinking, but "integral ecology." The integral approach runs throughout the encyclical. It is also the title of the fourth chapter of the encyclical. The opening paragraph of this chapter is programmatic and provides the essential constituents of the concept of integral ecology offered in the encyclical:

> Since everything is closely interrelated, and today's problems call for a vision capable of taking into account every aspect of the global crisis, I suggest that we now consider some elements of an *integral ecology*, one which clearly respects its human and social dimensions. (137)

In the footsteps of Pope Francis, we shall present the theme of integral ecology in *Laudato Si'* in the following manner. We will begin with a reflection on Pope Francis's affirmation "everything is closely interrelated" and will seek to make explicit the underlying relational metaphysics of the encyclical. According to the pope, "Today's problems call for a vision capable of taking into account every aspect of the global crisis." We will therefore examine how the integral approach of the encyclical makes possible not only a holistic understanding of the crisis of our common home but also a comprehensive response to it. We will then present the two essential and constitutive elements of integral ecology as indicated by the pope, namely, its "human and social dimensions." We will conclude with a brief mention of Saint Francis of Assisi as a model of integral ecology as proposed in the encyclical.

The Underlying Relational Metaphysics of Laudato Si'

What is the underlying metaphysics of the "integral ecology" of Pope Francis in *Laudato Si'*? It is the truth and conviction of the interrelatedness of the whole of reality and the interdependence of all created entities. "We are all connected" is the *mantra* that is repeated throughout the document.[1] We are connected to the rest of the human family, to the created world, and to those who will come after us in future generations. It is a sort of ontological glue that holds together the encyclical's main premises and arguments.

Already in the introduction to the encyclical, while enumerating the main themes of the text, Pope Francis speaks of "the conviction that everything in the world is connected" (16). The pope notes that the reality of the interconnectedness of all things is a revealed truth found in the very first chapters of the book of Genesis. While referring to the biblical episodes, he remarks: "These ancient stories, full of symbolism, bear witness to a conviction which we today share, that everything is interconnected, and that genuine care for our own

---

1. See in this regard Daniel R. DiLeo, ed., *All Creation Is Connected: Voices in Response to Pope Francis's Encyclical on Ecology* (Winona, MI: Anselm Academic, 2018); Vincent J. Miller, "Integral Ecology: Francis' Spiritual and Moral Vision of Interconnectedness," in *The Theological and Ecological Vision of Laudato Si': Everything Is Connected*, ed. Vincent J. Miller (London: Bloomsbury, 2017), 11–28.

lives and our relationships with nature is inseparable from fraternity, justice and faithfulness to others" (70).

The truth of the interdependence of all reality is the core of Christian belief and doctrine as affirmed by the *Catechism of the Catholic Church*, which the pope quotes in the encyclical:

> As the Catechism teaches: "God wills the interdependence of creatures. The sun and the moon, the cedar and the little flower, the eagle and the sparrow: the spectacle of their countless diversities and inequalities tells us that no creature is self-sufficient. Creatures exist only in dependence on each other, to complete each other, in the service of each other."[2] (86)

The metaphysical and anthropological vision of *Laudato Si'* is that we "human beings are not completely autonomous" (105). The pope points to the bonds of our cosmic, biological, and human fellowship, enwrapped in God's infinite love. "Everything is related, and we human beings are united as brothers and sisters on a wonderful pilgrimage, woven together by the love God has for each of his creatures and which also unites us in fond affection with brother sun, sister moon, brother river and mother earth" (92).

The metaphysics of interrelatedness is at the very heart of ecology that "studies the relationship between living organisms and the environment in which they develop" (138). The pope notes how interrelatedness and interdependence are the law of life on our home planet. Living species are to be understood only as "part of a network," "as the different aspects of the planet—physical, chemical and biological—are interrelated" (138). The truth of interrelatedness is particularly evident in the case of ecosystems. In the natural world "different creatures relate to one another in making up the

2. *Catechism of the Catholic Church*, 340.

larger units which today we term 'ecosystems.'" Ecosystems are basically the intricate interrelationship between species, "harmonious ensemble of organisms existing in a defined space and functioning as a system," so fundamental to sustain life on our home planet.

> Although we are often not aware of it, we depend on these larger systems for our own existence. We need only recall how ecosystems interact in dispersing carbon dioxide, purifying water, controlling illnesses and epidemics, forming soil, breaking down waste, and in many other ways which we overlook or simply ignore. Once they become conscious of this, many people realize that we live and act on the basis of a reality which has previously been given to us, which precedes our existence and our abilities. (140)

The metaphysical principle of interrelatedness and interdependence among creatures requires that we treat every creature with respect. "Because all creatures are connected, each must be cherished with love and respect, for all of us as living creatures are dependent on one another" (42). The pope also warns us to be careful not to rupture the seamless garb of the web of life, as it can lead to negative consequences. As Pope John Paul II noted in 1990, "We cannot interfere in one area of the ecosystem without paying due attention to the consequences of such interference in other areas"[3] (131).

The truth of interrelatedness and interdependence is also the ultimate metaphysical basis of all social life. It is the basis of our universal communion and of the universal destination of all goods. "As part of the universe, called into being by one Father, all of us are linked by unseen bonds and together form a kind of universal family" (89). We will dwell more on it later when dealing with the question of social ecology.

---

3. Pope John Paul II, *Message for the 1990 Word Day of Peace*, 6: *AAS* 82 (1990), 150.

The relational ontology of the interrelatedness of all created reality is ultimately based on the very relational nature of the Creator, the Source of all being. With profound insight, the pope points out in the encyclical how the fundamental theological foundation for the interrelatedness of all reality, of all forms of life, and of all social structures, is the very trinitarian communion, which has "left its mark on all creation" (239). John Bayer writes in this regard: "Against a worldview that privileges the autonomous and unattached individual, Pope Francis says that reality, a creation of the Holy Trinity, mirrors its Creator as a network of interdependent relations, as a locus of communion."[4]

The encyclical, in fact, ends by reminding us that "the divine Persons are subsistent relations, and the world, created according to the divine model, is a web of relationships." It is in living out our existence as communitarian beings, as interrelated and interdependent, that human beings find our true fulfillment, entering "into relationships, going out from themselves to live in communion with God, with others and with all creatures." "Global solidarity" thus ultimately "flows from the mystery of the Trinity" (240).

An Integral Approach in Understanding and Responding to the Crisis of Our Common Home

Pope Francis employs the integral approach in *Laudato Si'* both to understand and to respond to the crisis of our common home. Against occasional aberrations of some of the ecological movements in the past, which were passionately concerned

---

4. John Bayer, "A Voice Crying in the Desert: *Laudato Si'* as Prophecy," *The Way* 54 (2015), 79. See also Denis Edwards, " 'Everything Is Interconnected': The Trinity and the Natural World in *Laudato Si'*," *The Australasian Catholic Record* 94 (2017), 81–92.

about the plight of exotic species, while being callous about people dying of hunger, or were concerned about the preservation of pristine ecosystems, while remaining indifferent to indigenous communities who dwelt therein for millennia, the encyclical knits together a truly comprehensive understanding of the ecological crisis, its causes and possible solutions. Pope Francis is aware that the reductive epistemology of the modern technocratic paradigm is blind to the truth of interrelatedness and obscures the vision of the "larger picture." The crisis of our common home and of our common family is due precisely to the lack of a unitary vision and approach:

> The specialization which belongs to technology makes it difficult to see the larger picture. The fragmentation of knowledge proves helpful for concrete applications, and yet it often leads to a loss of appreciation for the whole, for the relationships between things, and for the broader horizon, which then becomes irrelevant. This very fact makes it hard to find adequate ways of solving the more complex problems of today's world, particularly those regarding the environment and the poor; these problems cannot be dealt with from a single perspective or from a single set of interests. A science which would offer solutions to the great issues would necessarily have to take into account the data generated by other fields of knowledge, including philosophy and social ethics; but this is a difficult habit to acquire today. (110)

The integral ecological approach of *Laudato Si'* is evident in its attention to combine insights from all branches of human wisdom: from natural and human sciences, from social and political sciences, from theological and philosophical disciplines. In the encyclical, Pope Francis opts for a dialogical and inclusive approach, integrating insights from various traditions, schools of thought, and individual thinkers. It is significant that the pope attempts to make a synthesis of what his predecessors as well as other religious leaders, local bishops' conferences, scientists, philosophers, theologians, sociologists, and others have said on the crisis of our common home and how we can care for it. He quotes from a wide range of sources, from the ecumenical patriarch Bartholomew to the Sufi mystic Ali al-Khawas, from Dante to Teilhard de Chardin.

The integral approach of *Laudato Si'* makes possible a holistic understanding of the crisis of our common home and a comprehensive response to it. Pope Francis offers, first of all, a holistic and integral understanding of the crisis of our common home. As he reminds us, we cannot treat "the environment in isolation; the issue cannot be approached piecemeal" (160). The integral approach is put into service also in the understanding of individual manifestations of the ecological crisis like climate change. While dealing with climate change, the encyclical points out that we are walking into a vicious cycle of impacts and causes:

> Warming has effects on the carbon cycle. It creates a vicious circle which aggravates the situation even more, affecting the availability of essential resources like drinking water, energy and agricultural production in warmer regions, and leading to the extinction of part of the planet's biodiversity. The melting in the polar ice caps and in high altitude plains can lead to the dangerous release of methane gas, while the decomposition of frozen organic material can further increase the emission of carbon dioxide. (24)

The way to overcome the crisis facing our common home also has to be integral and in keeping with the relational metaphysics of interdependence. According to Pope Francis, the truth of "interdependence obliges us to think *one world with a common plan*" (164). We also need comprehensive solutions.

"Given the scale of change, it is no longer possible to find a specific, discrete answer for each part of the problem. It is essential to seek comprehensive solutions which consider the interactions within natural systems themselves and with social systems" (139). The pope notes:

> Given the complexity of the ecological crisis and its mul-
> tiple causes we need to realize that the solutions will not
> emerge from just one way of interpreting and transforming
> reality. . . . If we are truly concerned to develop an ecol-
> ogy capable of remedying the damage we have done, no
> branch of the sciences and no form of wisdom can be left
> out. (63)

The pope therefore invites us to act at various levels as individuals and communities, at the local, regional, national, and international levels to respond to the crisis of our common home. We need to dialogue with all people of good will. Integral ecology demands that the protection of nature and the protection of the weaker members of our human family be seen as inextricably linked. The pope states that "strategies for a solution demand an integrated approach to combating poverty, restoring dignity to the excluded, and at the same time protecting nature" (139).

The integral approach adopted by Pope Francis in *Laudato Si'* necessitates that we widen the horizons of our talk of the ecological discourse. At times in the past, the ecological discourse ran the risk of being concerned mainly with the "environment" outside, often dealing with issues like the protection of exotic species and the conservation of pristine ecosystems. The pope reminds us in the encyclical that integral ecology essentially entails human and social dimensions. Pope Francis recalls a fundamental insight from Pope Benedict in this regard, namely, "that the world cannot be analyzed by isolating only one of its aspects, since 'the book of nature is one and indivisible,'[5] and includes the environment, life, sexuality, the family, social relations, and so forth" (6). Accordingly, any talk of the crisis of our common home and its healing needs to include humanity in the first place. It is the human and social dimensions of ecology on which we shall aim to reflect now.

Human Ecology

Human ecology is a term that was introduced by Pope John Paul II nearly a quarter of a century ago.[6] Pope Francis recovers this expression in *Laudato Si'* in the preamble to the text in order to establish the link between the degradation of our common planetary home and the deterioration of the human environment. According to him, "the destruction of the human environment is extremely serious, not only because God has entrusted the world to us men and women, but because human life is itself a gift which must be defended from various forms of debasement" (5).

The integral ecology of *Laudato Si'* is clearly evident in its conception of the human being who is at the same time both *imago mundi* (2) and *imago Dei* (65). Right at the beginning of the encyclical the pope reminds us that "we ourselves are dust of the earth (cf. Gen 2:7); our bodies are made up of her elements, we breathe her air and we receive life and refreshment from her waters" (2). At the same time, referring to the Genesis account of creation, the encyclical points out that "every man and woman is created out of love and made in

5. Pope Benedict XVI, Encyclical Letter *Caritas in Veritate* (29 June 2009), 51: *AAS* 101 (2009), 687.

6. John Paul II, Encyclical Letter *Centesimus Annus* (1 May 1991), 38: *AAS* 83 (1991), 841.

God's image and likeness (cf. Gen 1:26)" (65). On account of this profound truth, we have "our unique place as human beings in this world and our relationship to our surroundings" (15). Given the uniqueness of the human person in our common home, "there can be no renewal of our relationship with nature without a renewal of humanity itself" (118).

Pope Francis comments in *Laudato Si'* that the human environment is not only the natural world but also the concrete settings "in which people live their lives" and which "influence the way we think, feel and act" (147). The quality of human life suffers when these settings are degraded:

> In our rooms, our homes, our workplaces and neighbourhoods, we use our environment as a way of expressing our identity. We make every effort to adapt to our environment, but when it is disorderly, chaotic or saturated with noise and ugliness, such overstimulation makes it difficult to find ourselves integrated and happy. (147)

Pope Francis refers to the physical deterioration of human environments. For example, he speaks of the concrete problem of the lack of housing in many parts of the world and its negative consequences on the quality of people's lives. It is thus a serious problem for human ecology:

> Lack of housing is a grave problem in many parts of the world, both in rural areas and in large cities, since state budgets usually cover only a small portion of the demand. Not only the poor, but many other members of society as well, find it difficult to own a home. Having a home has much to do with a sense of personal dignity and the growth of families. This is a major issue for human ecology. (152)

The pope notes how "the extreme poverty experienced in areas lacking harmony, open spaces or potential for integration, can lead to incidents of brutality and to exploitation by criminal organizations" (149). In a similar way, "in the unstable neighbourhoods of megacities, the daily experience of overcrowding and social anonymity can create a sense of uprootedness which spawns antisocial behaviour and violence" (149).

However, the silver lining in the clouds is that in many situations the poor and simple people who are victims of such forms of environmental degradation become themselves protagonists for the promotion of authentic human ecology. Pope Francis writes: "Many people in these conditions are able to weave bonds of belonging and togetherness which convert overcrowding into an experience of community in which the walls of the ego are torn down and the barriers of selfishness overcome" (149). The pope speaks of a commendable human ecology on the part of the poor who become promoters of "a communitarian salvation":

> An admirable creativity and generosity is shown by persons and groups who respond to environmental limitations by alleviating the adverse effects of their surroundings and learning to live their lives amid disorder and uncertainty. . . . At times a commendable human ecology is practised by the poor despite numerous hardships. The feeling of asphyxiation brought on by densely populated residential areas is countered if close and warm relationships develop, if communities are created, if the limitations of the environment are compensated for in the interior of each person who feels held within a network of solidarity and belonging. In this way, any place can turn from being a hell on earth into the setting for a dignified life. (148)

Pope Francis then proceeds to speak of a deeper level of integral ecology, namely, the recognition of the moral law inscribed in our very human nature. Respect for the totality of nature presupposes respect for our own human nature. "Human ecology also implies another profound reality: the relationship between human life and the moral law, which is inscribed in our nature and is necessary for the creation of a more dignified environment" (155). He quotes in this regard Pope Benedict, who spoke of an "ecology of man," based precisely on the fact that "man too has a nature that he must respect and that he cannot manipulate at will"[7] (155).

An essential element of human ecology is the acceptance and care of our own physical bodies which establishes us "in a direct relationship with the environment and with other living beings" (155). It is also a precondition for a harmonious relationship with the natural world around us. The pope writes: "The acceptance of our bodies as God's gift is vital for welcoming and accepting the entire world as a gift from the Father and our common home, whereas thinking that we enjoy absolute power over our own bodies turns, often subtly, into thinking that we enjoy absolute power over creation" (155). Integral and authentic ecology requires that we accept our bodies in its unique and distinctive elements of femininity and masculinity. "In this way we can joyfully accept the specific gifts of another man or woman, the work of God the Creator, and find mutual enrichment. It is not a healthy attitude which would seek 'to cancel out sexual difference because it no longer knows how to confront it' "[8] (155).

We may conclude our reflections on human ecology arguing for a new and integral humanism: "We urgently need a humanism capable of bringing together the different fields of knowledge, including economics, in the service of a more integral and integrating vision" (141).

7. Benedict XVI, *Address to the German Bundestag*, Berlin (22 September 2011): *AAS* 103 (2011), 668.

8. Pope Francis, *Catechesis* (15 April 2015): *L'Osservatore Romano* (16 April 2015), 8.

Social Ecology

Integral ecology has an essential and indispensable social dimension to it. Since everything is connected, environmental concerns cannot be considered in isolation of social concerns. Within the framework of integral ecology, the protection of the natural world is intimately linked with other aspects of human existence like economy, social, political, and cultural life and has concrete implications for the common good. Pope Francis writes:

> When we speak of the "environment," what we really mean is a relationship existing between nature and the society which lives in it. Nature cannot be regarded as something separate from ourselves or as a mere setting in which we live. We are part of nature, included in it and thus in constant interaction with it. Recognizing the reasons why a given area is polluted requires a study of the workings of society, its economy, its behaviour patterns, and the ways it grasps reality. (139)

Given the social dimension of the ecological discourse, "the analysis of environmental problems cannot be separated from the analysis of human, family, work-related and urban contexts, nor from how individuals relate to themselves, which leads in turn to how they relate to others and to the environment" (141). The social organization of human communities has a direct influence on the environment and on the very quality of human life:

> If everything is related, then the health of a society's institutions has consequences for the environment and the quality of human life. "Every violation of solidarity and civic friendship harms the environment."[9] Moreover, what

9. Benedict XVI, *Caritas in Veritate*, 51: *AAS*, 687.

takes place in any one area can have a direct or indirect influence on other areas. Thus, for example, drug use in affluent societies creates a continual and growing demand for products imported from poorer regions, where behaviour is corrupted, lives are destroyed, and the environment continues to deteriorate. (142)

As Pope Francis reminds us, "We are faced not with two separate crises, one environmental and the other social, but rather with one complex crisis which is both social and environmental" (139). "Concern for the environment thus needs to be joined to a sincere love for our fellow human beings and an unwavering commitment to resolving the problems of society" (91). A society deaf to the cry of the poor will also be equally deaf to the cry of the mother Earth. The pope writes with a ring of indictment of our contemporary society:

When we fail to acknowledge as part of reality the worth of a poor person, a human embryo, a person with disabilities—to offer just a few examples—it becomes difficult to hear the cry of nature itself; everything is connected. Once the human being declares independence . . . the very foundations of our life begin to crumble. (117)

Integral ecology has serious implications in our dealings not only with the natural world but also with our fellow human beings, especially the most vulnerable among them. Pope Francis is forthright: "Since everything is interrelated, concern for the protection of nature is also incompatible with the justification of abortion. . . . 'If personal and social sensitivity toward the acceptance of the new life is lost, then other forms of acceptance that are valuable for society also wither away'"[10] (120).

10. Ibid., 663.

In *Laudato Si'*, Pope Francis further widens the concept of ecology in general, and of social ecology in particular, in speaking of a "cultural ecology." The ecological crisis is linked also with the cultural crisis of our times. In our days, as the pope writes, "together with the patrimony of nature, there is also an historic, artistic and cultural patrimony which is likewise under threat" (143). We are witnessing, along with the destruction of species and ecosystems, the disappearance of cultures and traditions. As the pope notes, "The disappearance of a culture can be just as serious, or even more serious, than the disappearance of a species of plant or animal" (145).

Pope Francis singles out in this regard the tragic plight of indigenous communities in many parts of the world, who continue to be evicted from their ancestral homelands often under the disguise of developmental projects:

> In this sense, it is essential to show special care for indigenous communities and their cultural traditions. They are not merely one minority among others, but should be the principal dialogue partners, especially when large projects affecting their land are proposed. . . . When they remain on their land, they themselves care for it best. Nevertheless, in various parts of the world, pressure is being put on them to abandon their homelands to make room for agricultural or mining projects which are undertaken without regard for the degradation of nature and culture. (146)

Ecological protection thus necessarily involves the preservation and promotion of the cultural heritage of local human communities. According to Pope Francis, there is a need to respect the rights of peoples and cultures and elicit "active involvement of local people *from within their proper culture*" (144).

Saint Francis as the Model of Integral Ecology

For Pope Francis, the model of integral ecology is Saint Francis of Assisi himself, for his love for creation, love for the poor, and love for the Creator; the triple loves merged into a sublime unity:

> I believe that Saint Francis is the example par excellence of care for the vulnerable and of an integral ecology lived out joyfully and authentically. . . . He shows us how just inseparable the bond is between concern for nature, justice for the poor, commitment to society, and interior peace. (10)

Francis helps us to see that an integral ecology calls for openness to categories which transcend the language of mathematics and biology and take us to the heart of what it is to be human (11).

Francis of Assisi is at times reduced to an idealized nature mystic, in whom many modern eco-warriors find inspiration. Obviously, this is simplistic. The conversion of young Francis was indeed a triple conversion: to the whole of creation, to the poor, and ultimately to the very Creator. Francis's life—simple, compassionate, and saintly—is indeed a beautiful example of integral ecology for our times.[11]

11. See Joshtrom Isaac Kureethadam, *Creation in Crisis: Science, Ethics, Theology* (New York: Orbis, 2014), 371.

GREEN COMMANDMENT VII

Learn a New Way of Dwelling in Our Common Home

Our seventh green commandment is about a new way of dwelling in our common home. Given the global character of the ecological crisis, the involvement and dedication of the entire human community is needed to protect the earth. Pope Francis proposes various levels of our involvement in this regard, which range from the international to the national and the local. He also points out, in the spirit of eco-justice, that various nations and communities have a common but differentiated responsibility when it comes to responding to the crisis of our common home. According to the pope, the root causes of the crisis of our common home are to be found in current social and economic systems.[1] He therefore proposes a new way of managing our planetary home—a new economics—and a new way of governing our public institutions—a new political culture. We need a new economy, not one which is built on the myth of infinite growth and excludes the poor, but one which *respects* the cycles of nature and is at

---

1. Venugopalan Ittekkot and Eleanor Milne, "Encyclical Letter 'Laudato Si': A Gentle But Firm Nudge from Pope Francis," *Environmental Development* 17 (2016), 1.

the service of the whole of humanity. We will need new politics, not subservient to economic interests and power lobbies,
but at the service of the common good. We shall now proceed
to a detailed examination of these elements.

Acting Together as a Global Community to Care for Our Common Home

The main purpose of *Laudato Si'* is to motivate humanity
to act decisively to save our common home for ourselves and
for future generations. "The effects of the present imbalance
can only be reduced by our decisive action, here and now"
(161). As we are all one interdependent family, we need a
common plan to avert the threat to our common habitat.
"Interdependence obliges us to think of *one world with a common plan*" (164). The pope also reminds us that "all of us can
cooperate as instruments of God for the care of creation, each
according to his or her own culture, experience, involvements
and talents" (14).

In *Laudato Si'*, Pope Francis highlights the role of the international community in the protection of our common home.
He offers a synthetic overview of what has been done so far,
pointing out some conspicuous failures as well as some measured successes of the past. The pope also refers to some
limited successes in the arena of ecological protection on the
part of the international community. He mentions the Basel
Convention on hazardous wastes, the Convention on international trade in endangered species of wild fauna and flora,
the Vienna Convention for the protection of the ozone layer
which was subsequently implemented through the famous
Montreal Protocol (168). However, Pope Francis notes that
real successes in the efforts of the international community
to address serious problems facing our common planetary
home have been too few in the recent decades: "Recent World

Summits on the environment have not lived up to expectations because, due to lack of political will, they were unable to reach truly meaningful and effective global agreements on the environment" (166).

Pope Francis proceeds to indicate some guidelines, mainly ethical, for common action at the international level for the protection of our common planetary home. While referring to negotiations to mitigate climate change, the pope refers to the important principle of common but differentiated responsibilities enshrined in the *United Nations Framework Convention on Climate Change*. In *Laudato Si'*, Pope Francis raises his moral voice in defence of the poorer countries who risk burdensome commitments to reducing greenhouse gas emissions:

> Imposing such measures penalizes those countries most in need of development. A further injustice is perpetrated under the guise of protecting the environment. Here also, the poor end up paying the price. . . . In this context, there is a need for common and differentiated responsibilities. As the bishops of Bolivia have stated, "the countries which have benefited from a high degree of industrialization, at the cost of enormous emissions of greenhouse gases, have a greater responsibility for providing a solution to the problems they have caused."[2] (170)

As the pope states in the encyclical, the poor countries should not be coerced at the High Table of international negotiations on climate change to accept emission reduction targets that will affect their struggles to overcome the misery of many of their fellow citizens. For poor countries, the priority "must be to eliminate extreme poverty and to promote the

---

2. Bolivian Bishops' Conference, Pastoral Letter on the Environment and Human Development in Bolivia *El universo, don de Dios para la vida* (March 2012), 86.

social development of their people" (172). We need to combine protection of the natural world with the goal of eliminating poverty. "A more responsible overall approach is needed to deal with both problems: the reduction of pollution and the development of poorer countries and regions" (175).

Pope Francis points to the need of poorer nations to develop less polluting forms of energy production like solar energy and affirms that "to do so they require the help of countries which have experienced great growth at the cost of the ongoing pollution of the planet." Such an assistance would mean "the establishment of mechanisms and subsidies which allow developing countries access to technology transfer, technical assistance and financial resources." According to the pope, "these are primarily ethical decisions, rooted in solidarity between all peoples" (172).

The pope calls for international agreement and governance on a whole range of so-called "global commons" like the oceans, the problem of marine waste (174). "Global regulatory norms are needed to impose obligations and prevent unacceptable actions, for example, when powerful companies dump contaminated waste or offshore polluting industries in other countries" (173). He writes: "A global consensus is essential for confronting the deeper problems, which cannot be resolved by unilateral actions on the part of individual countries" (164).

In the safeguarding of our common home and in promoting the welfare of humanity and the rest of the biotic community, people can and must contribute also at national and local levels. As the pope states, "Individual states can no longer ignore their responsibility for planning, coordination, oversight and enforcement within their respective borders" of environmental initiatives and laws in defence of our common planetary home (177). The pope also sees room for creativity and positive action in this regard: "Political and institutional frameworks do not exist simply to avoid bad

practice, but also to promote best practice, to stimulate creativity in seeking new solutions and to encourage individual
or group initiatives" (177).

Pope Francis makes a special mention of the important
contribution of local ecological movements and many organizations of civil society around the world for the protection
of our common home:

> Society is also enriched by a countless array of organiza-
> tions which work to promote the common good and to
> defend the environment, whether natural or urban. Some,
> for example, show concern for a public place (a building,
> a fountain, an abandoned monument, a landscape, a
> square), and strive to protect, restore, improve or beautify
> it as something belonging to everyone. Around these com-
> munity actions, relationships develop or are recovered and
> a new social fabric emerges. (232)

Laudato Si' is clearly intended to influence and shape the
international debate about the care of our common home and
generate a paradigm shift over the long term.[3] We can only
hope that this truly happens.

Toward a New Economy to Manage Our Common Home

Apart from specific actions on the part of humanity at
international, national, and local levels for the stewardship
of Earth, what is needed is a radically new way of managing
our common home. We need nothing short of a new economy.
Economics is not primarily about making profit. It is essentially *Wirtschaft* as the Germans would say, handling or taking
care, as an innkeeper would do, of the proper habitat; it is

---

3. Jeffrey Mazo, "The Pope's Divisions," *Survival* 57/4 (2015), 209.

Haushalt, governing, managing, one's own household. This is also the Greek etymological meaning of the term economics (*oikos* + *nomos*), namely, the law or rule of one's household. Today, in the context of the contemporary ecological crisis, economics needs to reinterpret itself as the art and science of managing our common planetary home.

The precarious state of our common home has to do largely with the *mis*management of it in the recent past, guided by false economic theories. The overarching belief that guides modern economic capitalism is that nature is merely a storehouse of resources to be utilized for human consumption. Accordingly the natural world gets reduced to a heap of commodities, meticulously calculated in terms of their monetary value, to be used, stored, and bartered. "Nature takes on a single meaning, that of 'resource' or 'raw material' for human exploitation and use."[4] A quantitative paradigm in the perception of nature continues to condition contemporary social values and thinking, as nations and societies come to be valued in terms of GNP, and development is seen in terms of capacity to exploit and utilize the resources of the earth.

In *Laudato Si'*, Pope Francis is critical of modern economics precisely for its one-dimensional view of the natural world as a storehouse of resources for human consumption and isolated from social and environmental concerns. He writes:

> The principle of the maximization of profits, frequently isolated from other considerations, reflects a misunderstanding of the very concept of the economy. As long as production is increased, little concern is given to whether it is at the cost of future resources or the health of the environment; as long as the clearing of a forest increases production, no one calculates the losses entailed in the desertification of the land, the harm done to biodiversity or the increased pollution. In

---

4. David Toolan, *At Home in the Cosmos* (New York: Orbis, 2001), 43–44.

a word, businesses profit by calculating and paying only a
fraction of the costs involved. (195)

According to the pope, current free market economic theories are totally inadequate for the protection of our common
planetary home. Pope Francis reiterates in this regard Pope
Benedict's affirmation in *Caritas in veritate*: "By itself the market cannot guarantee integral human development and social
inclusion"[5] (109). Market economy is totally inadequate for
the protection of the natural world and safeguarding the
needs of the poor:

> We need to reject a magical conception of the market, which
> would suggest that problems can be solved simply by an
> increase in the profits of companies or individuals. Is it
> realistic to hope that those who are obsessed with maximiz-
> ing profits will stop to reflect on the environmental damage
> which they will leave behind for future generations? Where
> profits alone count, there can be no thinking about the
> rhythms of nature, its phases of decay and regeneration,
> or the complexity of ecosystems which may be gravely
> upset by human intervention. Moreover, biodiversity is
> considered at most a deposit of economic resources avail-
> able for exploitation, with no serious thought for the real
> value of things, their significance for persons and cultures,
> or the concerns and needs of the poor. (190)

The current economic system largely excludes the poor
and vulnerable sections of society. Globalization along with
its "economy of exclusion"[6] has *left hundreds of millions of*

5. Cf. Pope Benedict XVI, Encyclical Letter *Caritas in Veritate* (29 June
2009), 35: *AAS* 101 (2009), 671.

6. Pope Francis, Apostolic Exhortation *Evangelii Gaudium* (24 November 2013), 53–54.

people behind: 1.2 billion lack access to electricity, 870 million are malnourished, and at least 748 million are without access to clean, safe drinking water.[7] The world economy grew twentyfold in the last century alone.[8] It is creating wealth at a scale and a breadth never before experienced. At the same time it is also generating unprecedented levels of overall inequality.[9] It is clear that economic growth has not benefited everyone in society equally. Significant inequalities remain and many of the most vulnerable groups in society have been left behind. Pope Francis sees ecology, economy, and equity as inextricably interlinked.[10]

Today, we stand in need of a new "ecological" economics, respectful of the ecosystems and natural cycles of the planetary home where we dwell and at the service of the whole of humanity. As Anthony Annett rightly remarks, "The economic vision of Pope Francis is a human vision."[11] The pope indicates that we need "an 'economic ecology' capable of appealing to a broader vision of reality" (141). In keeping with the spirit of the integral ecology of *Laudato Si'*, Pope Francis quotes the *Rio Declaration on Environment and Development*: "The protection of the environment is in fact 'an integral

7. Data from World Bank: http://www.worldbank.org/mdgs/environment.html (accessed on 7 February 2015).

8. See Angus Maddison, *The World Economy: Historical Statistics* (Paris: OECD, 2004); UNEP, *Global Environment Outlook 5: Environment for the Future of All* (Nairobi: UNEP, 2012), 5.

9. Tim O'Riordan et al., "The Legacy of the Papal Encyclical," *Environment: Science and Policy for Sustainable Development* 57/6 (2015), 2.

10. Mary Evelyn Tucker, "Ecological Challenges Evoke Ethical Response," *Environment: Science and Policy for Sustainable Development* 57/6 (2015), 25.

11. Anthony Annett, "The Economic Vision of Pope Francis," in *The Theological and Ecological Vision of Laudato Si': Everything Is Connected*, ed. Vincent J. Miller (London: Bloomsbury, 2017), 160.

part of the development process and cannot be considered in isolation from it.'[12] We urgently need a humanism capable of bringing together the different fields of knowledge, including economics, in the service of a more integral and integrating vision" (141).

Ecological economics rejects the myth of infinite growth which is considers sacrosanct in the reigning economic paradigm and which is also one of the main factors contributing to the pillage of our common home. Pope Francis criticizes the easy acceptance of "the idea of infinite or unlimited growth, which proves so attractive to economists, financiers and experts in technology. It is based on the lie that there is an infinite supply of earth's goods, and this leads to the planet being squeezed dry beyond every limit" (106). It is time to think of containing exponential economic growth or even promoting a sort of de-growth for the highly advanced economies, so that poorer communities can achieve the required economic growth for a dignified existence. Pope Francis writes in this regard, drawing inspiration from Pope Benedict:

> In any event, if in some cases sustainable development were to involve new forms of growth, in other cases, given the insatiable and irresponsible growth produced over many decades, we need also to think of containing growth by setting some reasonable limits and even retracing our steps before it is too late. We know how unsustainable is the behaviour of those who constantly consume and destroy, while others are not yet able to live in a way worthy of their human dignity. That is why the time has come to accept decreased growth in some parts of the world, in order to provide resources for other places to experience healthy growth. Benedict XVI has said that "technologically

---

12. *Rio Declaration on Environment and Development* (14 June 1992), Principle 4.

advanced societies must be prepared to encourage more sober lifestyles, while reducing their energy consumption and improving its efficiency."[13] (193)

According to the pope, a reorientation of economy calls for "redefining our notion of progress" (194). The social nature of ecology "necessarily entails reflection and debate about the conditions required for the life and survival of society, and the honesty needed to question certain models of development, production and consumption" (138). So "a technological and economic development which does not leave in its wake a better world and an integrally higher quality of life cannot be considered progress" (194).

Pope Francis criticizes our current throwaway culture and notes with regret that we have not yet arrived at a "circular" model of economic production, imitating the example provided by nature:

> It is hard for us to accept that the way natural ecosystems work is exemplary: plants synthesize nutrients which feed herbivores; these in turn become food for carnivores, which produce significant quantities of organic waste which give rise to new generations of plants. But our industrial system, at the end of its cycle of production and consumption, has not developed the capacity to absorb and reuse waste and by-products. We have not yet managed to adopt a circular model of production capable of preserving resources for present and future generations, while limiting as much as possible the use of non-renewable resources, moderating their consumption, maximizing their efficient use, reusing and recycling them. (22)

---

13. Benedict XVI, *Message for the 2010 World Day of Peace*, 9: *AAS* 102 (2010), 46.

Pope Francis's courageous invitation to move away from fossil fuels to renewable forms of energy deserves special mention, given that today the world energy needs depend nearly 80 percent on fossil fuels, which are the greatest contributors to global warming. The pope affirms clearly: "We know that technology based on the use of highly polluting fossil fuels—especially coal, but also oil and, to a lesser degree, gas—needs to be progressively replaced without delay." He also notes with concern that "the international community has still not reached adequate agreements about the responsibility for paying the costs of this energy transition" (165). In spite of the immediate costs of such a transition, the pope points out their real costs "would be low, compared to the risks of climate change" (172).

As Naomi Klein has pointed out, "Our economic system and our planetary system are now at war."[14] The contemporary ecological crisis, the crisis of our common home, is a stark reminder of this truth and a loud clarion call to create a new way of managing the Earth. Klein writes: "It is a civilizational wake-up call. A powerful message—spoken in the language of fires, floods, droughts, and extinctions—telling us we need an entirely new economic model and a new way of sharing this planet."[15]

For a new economics, understood as the art of managing our common planetary home, an adequate political culture is also vitally important. As Pope Francis states, "Economics without politics cannot be justified" (196). It is to the new political culture needed to manage our common home that we turn our attention now.

---

14. Naomi Klein, *This Changes Everything: Capitalism vs. the Climate* (London: Penguin Books, 2015), 21.

15. Ibid., 25.

A New Political Culture for the Care
of Our Common Planetary Home

In the context of the contemporary ecological crisis, ensuring the habitability of our common planetary home becomes
the most important of all common goods, as it is a necessary
precondition for the fulfillment of the rest. Here politics
whose primary vocation is to serve the common good has an
important and indispensable role to play.

In *Laudato Si'*, Pope Francis is critical of the present political
culture in relation to the protection of the natural environment within which human societies exist. Present-day politics, according to the pope, often lacks a long-term view of
environmental protection, as it is mostly driven by the consumerist trend for immediate gratification. As he writes, the
culture of consumerism "prioritizes short-term gain and private interest" (184) which does not facilitate far-sighted policies for the protection of our common home:

> A politics concerned with immediate results, supported by
> consumerist sectors of the population, is driven to produce
> short-term growth. In response to electoral interests, gov-
> ernments are reluctant to upset the public with measures
> which could affect the level of consumption or create risks
> for foreign investment. The myopia of power politics de-
> lays the inclusion of a far-sighted environmental agenda
> within the overall agenda of governments. (178)

A major problem with politics today, notes Pope Francis,
is that it is too subservient to economic interests. Such a situation is a real stumbling block for efforts to resolve ecological
problems around the world. Referring to the failure of international summits on climate change hitherto, Pope Francis
attributes them to such "powerful interests" (50). "There are
too many special interests and economic interests . . . trump-
ing the common good and manipulating information so that
their own plans will not be affected" (54).

Pope Francis criticizes in particular the strangling hold of multinational companies over political structures. "The twenty-first century, while maintaining systems of governance inherited from the past, is witnessing a weakening of the power of nation states, chiefly because the economic and financial sectors, being transnational, tends to prevail over the political" (175). As the pope points out, some of these economic entities "exercise more power than states themselves" (196). They have indeed come to assume unprecedented power in the global political and economic spheres.

Against the current political culture which is subservient to vested economic interests and contributes to the ravaging of our common planetary home, Pope Francis calls for a politics at the service of the common good: "Society as a whole, and the state in particular, are obliged to defend and promote the common good" (157). The principle of subsidiarity, well enshrined in the Catholic social teachings, demands "a greater sense of responsibility for the common good from those who wield greater power" (196). The pope calls for a new political culture which is farsighted and radical:

> What is needed is a politics which is farsighted and capable of a new, integral and interdisciplinary approach to handling the different aspects of the crisis. . . . A strategy for real change calls for rethinking processes in their entirety, for it is not enough to include a few superficial ecological considerations while failing to question the logic which underlies present-day culture. (197)

Pope Francis insists on "the inclusion of a far-sighted environmental agenda within the overall agenda of governments. . . . True statecraft is manifest when, in difficult times, we uphold high principles and think of the long-term common good" (178). The pope goes on to explain that a long-term perspective is vital to resolving the crises facing our common home. "Continuity is essential, because policies related to climate change and environmental protection cannot be altered with every change of government" (181).

Given the global character of the contemporary ecological crisis, Pope Francis calls for "a true world political authority," renewing an appeal that was already made by his predecessors Pope John XXIII and Pope Benedict XVI.[16] We need such a global institution "to manage the global economy; to revive economies hit by the crisis; to avoid any deterioration of the present crisis and the greater imbalances that would result; to bring about integral and timely disarmament, food security and peace; to guarantee the protection of the environment and to regulate migration" (175). According to the pope, we need "stronger and more efficiently organized international institutions, with functionaries who are appointed fairly by agreement among national governments, and empowered to impose sanctions" (175). On the other hand, it is important to ensure that local communities "have a special place at the table; they are concerned about their own future and that of their children, and can consider goals transcending immediate economic interest" (183).

As Pope Francis affirms in the encyclical, politics has an indispensable role to play in efforts to protect our common home: "Unless citizens control political power—national, regional and municipal—it will not be possible to control damage to the environment" (179).

The Wider Horizon of the Common Good

A clear criteria that Pope Francis proposes in *Laudato Si'*, in line with the Catholic social teachings, is that both politics and economics should be at the service of the common good and of human life in particular. He writes:

16. Benedict XVI, *Caritas in Veritate*, 67.

Politics must not be subject to the economy, nor should the economy be subject to the dictates of an efficiency-driven paradigm of technocracy. Today, in view of the common good, there is urgent need for politics and economics to enter into a frank dialogue in the service of life, especially human life. (189)

In *Laudato Si'*, Pope Francis recalls the definition of the common good on the part of the Second Vatican Council as "the sum of those conditions of social life which allow social groups and their individual members relatively thorough and ready access to their own fulfilment"[17] (156). Pope Francis echoes in the encyclical the fundamental principle in Vatican II's document *Gaudium et Spes*: "God has destined the earth and everything it contains for all peoples and all nations"[18] (cf. 158). Only the tireless and dedicated pursuit of the common good can protect our planetary home and its most vulnerable inhabitants.

As Pope Francis notes in *Laudato Si'*, "The notion of the common good also extends to future generations, . . . those who come after us. We can no longer speak of sustainable development apart from intergenerational solidarity. Once we start to think about the kind of world we are leaving to future generations, we look at things differently; we realize that the world is a gift which we have freely received and must share with others" (159).

The greatest of all common goods is our common planetary home where we live as a common family with our fellow human beings and the rest of the biotic community. Its care and protection become a real common good to be pursued on the part of humanity in our current era of planetary crisis.

17. Second Vatican Ecumenical Council, Pastoral Constitution on the Church in the Modern World *Gaudium et Spes*, 26.
18. Ibid., 69.

GREEN COMMANDMENT VIII

Educate toward Ecological Citizenship

The care of our imperiled common planetary home calls for a profound renewal of our lifestyles. It is a huge challenge awaiting humanity. As Pope Francis affirms: "A great cultural, spiritual and educational challenge stands before us, and it will demand that we set out on the long path of renewal" (202). The last chapter of the encyclical is rightly dedicated to ecological education and spirituality which are like the two wings that can enable the human person to take off on the lifelong journey of ecological conversion.

Our eighth green commandment is about ecological education, while the question of ecological spirituality will be taken up in the next one. As the crisis of our common home is caused by human activities, we stand in need of a radical change in our consumption-driven lifestyles which are taking a heavy toll on the sustainability of our planetary home. Such deep changes can be brought about only through education. In the encyclical, Pope Francis calls for a rethinking of environmental education to create a new covenant between humanity and the natural world. We need a holistic education that can reestablish harmony with nature, our fellow human beings, and the Transcendent. The pope also speaks of the variety of settings for ecological education: schools, families, media, catechesis, houses of religious formation. We will conclude with a note on the importance of education for ecological citizenship in this crucial moment of our planetary emergency.

The Challenge of New Lifestyles against Rampant Consumerism

The precarious state of our common home today demands that we be courageous to choose lifestyles which are "countercultural" (108). Given the gravity of the crisis, simple solutions like a bit of recycling or occasional bicycling will not do. As Mark Dowd writes: "We should not fool ourselves into thinking that 'deckchair-rearranging' activities such as giving up plastic bags and changing light bulbs will be enough to put the tanker that is environmental degradation off course."[1] We need nothing short of radically new lifestyles if we are to save our common planetary home for ourselves and for future generations.

In order to save our common home, we will need to overcome especially our addiction to profligate consumption, so widespread in economically advanced societies and spreading like wildfire to the rest of the world with the globalization of the current neoliberal economic model. Such lifestyles of excessive consumption, especially on the part of the rich and affluent sections of society, are depleting the natural resources of our common household. As the pope notes in the encyclical, we are the victims of compulsive consumerism which is also a principal source of anxiety for the postmodern humanity:

---

1. Mark Dowd, "For Every Living Creature on Earth," *The Tablet* (13 June 2015), 4.

Since the market tends to promote extreme consumerism in
an effort to sell its products, people can easily get caught up
in a whirlwind of needless buying and spending. Compulsive consumerism is one example of how the techno-
economic paradigm affects individuals. . . . This paradigm
leads people to believe that they are free as long as they have
the supposed freedom to consume. But those really free are
the minority who wield economic and financial power. Amid
this confusion, postmodern humanity has not yet achieved
a new self-awareness capable of offering guidance and direction, and this lack of identity is a source of anxiety. (203)

Our levels of rapacious consumption are indeed pillaging
our common planetary home. The consumption of many
important natural resources is clearly beyond their renewal
capacity rates. In the case of important natural sources like
fisheries, forests, biodiversity, and especially fresh water, we
are fast approaching crucial thresholds. In the epoch of the
Holocene, and during most of the last 6,000 years since civilization began, we have lived on the sustainable yield of the
Earth's natural systems. But in recent decades, it appears that
we are overshooting the capacity of our home planet's natural
resources that sustain us. In fact, the popular and widely used
mechanism of the Ecological Footprint Analysis clearly shows
an alarming trend of overconsumption. Currently, humanity
as a whole consumes, or rather over-consumes, 1.5 planets a
year and the situation is projected to get even worse in the
future, given current levels of consumption and waste.[2]

The rapid depletion of our home planet's natural resources
in blissful ignorance of the larger ecological context is a sure
recipe for global disaster. As Seán McDonagh notes: "The
Earth's ledger, which in the final analysis is the only real one,

2. See in this regard Global Footprint Network et al., *Living Planet
Report 2014: Species and Spaces, People and Places* (Gland: WWF, 2014), 9.

tells us that the Earth is finite and vulnerable, and that natural systems will be seriously depleted and possibly collapse unless human beings begin to shape their lives in the light of this reality of ecological accounting."[3] No previous generation has survived the ongoing destruction of its natural supports. Nor will ours.

Laudato Si' makes a profound critique of the "throwaway culture" of which we are all a part.[4] The encyclical is a clear condemnation of the culture of greed and materialism, exemplified in the so-called shopping culture of our times.[5] In the encyclical, Pope Francis also offers an attentive diagnosis about the roots of our reckless consumption patterns:

> When people become self-centred and self-enclosed, their greed increases. The emptier a person's heart is, the more he or she needs things to buy, own and consume. It becomes almost impossible to accept the limits imposed by reality. In this horizon, a genuine sense of the common good also disappears. As these attitudes become more widespread, social norms are respected only to the extent that they do not clash with personal needs. So our concern cannot be limited merely to the threat of extreme weather events, but must also extend to the catastrophic consequences of social unrest. Obsession with a consumerist lifestyle, above all when few people are capable of maintaining it, can only lead to violence and mutual destruction. (204)

Against such unhealthy consumption patterns that tear down the physical and social pillars of our common home,

---

3. Seán McDonagh, *To Care for the Earth: A Call to a New Theology* (London: Geoffrey Chapman, 1986), 45.

4. John D. Wilsey, "Whose Land?," *America* (November 28, 2016), 20.

5. See Susan Jacobson, Bill Weis, and Abigail B. Schneider, "*Laudato Si'* and the Consumption Challenge: Giving Students a Visceral Exercise in Saving Our Planet," *Jesuit Higher Education: A Journal* 6 (2017), 88.

Pope Francis calls for a radical "change in lifestyle" which "could bring healthy pressure to bear on those who wield political, economic and social power. . . . 'The issue of environmental degradation challenges us to examine our lifestyle' "[6] (206).

How can we develop a different lifestyle in order to bring about significant changes in society and save our common planetary home? In *Laudato Si'*, Pope Francis suggests that education has a vital role to play in this important task. It is to the role of education in ushering in a radically new and harmonious relationship with our common home that we turn now.

Rethinking Ecological Education for a New Covenant with Our Planetary Home

According to Pope Francis, in the context of the imminent collapse of our common home and the increasing breakdown of social relationships, "we are faced with an educational challenge" (209). Education is the path on which to accompany all, especially young people, to become responsible stewards of our common home. In this critical moment of planetary civilization, the silver lining in the clouds is that young people are increasingly becoming real protagonists of efforts to protect and preserve our common planetary home. However, as they live in an atmosphere of excessive consumerism, they need to be helped to cultivate more sustainable lifestyles. The pope writes:

6. Pope Benedict XVI, *Message for the 2010 World Day of Peace*, 11: *AAS* 102 (2010), 48. See in this regard also Daniel R. DiLeo, "Creation Care through Consumption and Life Choices," in *The Theological and Ecological Vision of Laudato Si': Everything Is Connected*, ed. Vincent J. Miller (London: Bloomsbury, 2017), 217–34.

In those countries which should be making the greatest
changes in consumer habits, young people have a new
ecological sensitivity and a generous spirit, and some of
them are making admirable efforts to protect the environment. At the same time, they have grown up in a milieu of
extreme consumerism and affluence which makes it difficult to develop other habits. (209)

Young people are most vulnerable to the contemporary
consumerist culture, but they can also be guided to make
responsible ecological choices in terms of lifestyles. We are
thus faced with a challenge as well as an opportunity in the
area of environmental education. Pope Francis notes how
"environmental education has broadened its goals." He refers
to some of the new trends in environmental education:
"Whereas in the beginning it was mainly centred on scientific
information, consciousness-raising and the prevention of
environmental risks, it tends now to include a critique of the
"myths" of a modernity grounded in a utilitarian mindset
(individualism, unlimited progress, competition, consumerism, the unregulated market)" (210).

The deeper sources of the utilitarian mind-set character-
ized by individualism and consumerism are modern anthropocentrism and the mechanistic vision of the natural world.
As noted educationists like C. A. Bowers, David W. Orr, and
others have pointed out, most of our current educational
systems are based on these presuppositions inherited from
modernity, anthropocentrism, and the mechanistic conception of nature, in particular. Modern anthropocentrism subtly
permeates educational curricula in most parts of the world.[7]

7. C. A. Bowers provides an excellent review of how anthropocentrism subtly permeates educational curricula as in the case of school
textbooks. See C. A. Bowers, *Education, Cultural Myths and the Ecological
Crisis: Toward Deep Changes* (Albany, NY: State University of New York
Press, 1993), 117–53.

According to Bowers, the main cultural message propagated by the contemporary educational system is the western myth that accords human beings the status of independence and absolute centrality in relation to other forms of life within biotic communities. He writes: "In all public education students encounter in textbooks an image of the individual as an autonomous agent engaged in social and technological activities. The pronoun 'you' is ubiquitous from grade one through grade twelve."[8] Modern and contemporary forms of educational theories and praxis are largely centered around the atomistic and reductive concept of the self, inherited from modernity.

Modern educational curricula also continue to transmit the mechanistic conception of the natural world inherited from modernity and indirectly subscribe to the instrumental rationality of modern industrial economy. In most textbooks, Earth is represented more as a source of natural resources for human consumption rather than a home that hosts and sustains humanity along with myriads of others forms of·life. The educational curricula and system mostly continue to work within a *Weltbild* or framework of unlimited economic expansion based on the myth of the infinite plenitude of natural resources and people as consumers.[9] Some of the top-notch centers of higher education continue to spawn engineers, technicians, and managers who measure their career success in terms of increased economic output, even at the cost of the well-being of the planet, and profit margins, even when it means depletion of the life-sustaining resources of our home planet and our common ecosystems. As David Orr points out, the ecological crisis is not caused mainly by ignorant people, but by those who are literate (people with BAs, BSs, LLBs, MBAs and PhDs), some of the best educated

8. Ibid., 125.
9. See ibid., 3, 127–30.

people in society.[10] According to Orr, the main focus of current educational curricula appears mostly to prepare the students to compete in the world economy as economic growth is presented as the highest goal.[11]

The underlying assumption of most environmental education curricula is that a bit of recycling, organic farming, occasional use of renewable forms of energy is all that it takes to ward off the ecological crisis, without having to fundamentally question our current mind-set and radically alter profligate consumerist lifestyles. As John Hilcoat and Eureta Janse van Rensburg point out, there exists a conspicuous "silence about malconsumption in environmental education."[12]

Pope Francis states that the new ecological culture needed to care for our common home "cannot be reduced to a series of urgent and practical responses to the immediate problems of pollution, environmental decay and the depletion of natural resources" (111). The changes required are much wider and far-reaching. "We need to develop a new synthesis capable of overcoming the false arguments of recent centuries" (121). "We urgently need a humanism capable of bringing together the different fields of knowledge" (141). What is required is a new vision of reality, a new way of conceiving our relationship with our common home. According to the pope, "There needs to be a distinctive way of looking at things, a way of thinking, policies, an educational programme, a lifestyle and a spirituality which together generate resistance to the assault of the technocratic paradigm" (111).

10. David W. Orr, *Earth in Mind: On Education, Environment and the Human Prospect* (Washington, DC: Island Press, 1994), 7.

11. Ibid., 16.

12. John Hilcoat and Eureta Janse van Rensburg, "Consuming Passions: Educating the Empty Self," *Australian Journal of Environmental Education* 30/1 (2014), 88.

A Holistic Understanding of Ecological Education

In *Laudato Si'*, Pope Francis proposes a holistic model of ecological education, capable of reestablishing harmony with nature, with others and with God: "It [ecological education] seeks also to restore the various levels of ecological equilibrium, establishing harmony within ourselves, with others, with nature and other living creatures, and with God" (210).

It is important to reflect on the holistic model of education proposed by Pope Francis in *Laudato Si'*, which is also in line with the integral ecology of the encyclical. Holistic education should lead to a peaceful coexistence with the natural world, our fellow human beings, and ultimately our very Creator. Let us go on to reflect briefly on each of these constitutive dimensions of ecological education.

Ecological education should help, first of all, to reestablish an intimate link with the natural world, our common home. Unfortunately, current educational curricula reinforce the modern worldview that humans are totally separate from the natural world and are not dependent on the web of biological ecosystems that sustain all life, including human life, on Earth. As F. Berkes and others have noted, our alienation from nature is a key component of environmental destruction.[13] Education toward sustainability requires a radical correction of such a "persistent and problematic 'human versus nature' binary,"[14] if we are to overcome our current ecological hazards.[15] A holistic educational curriculum educates students

13. See F. Berkes, *Sacred Ecology: Traditional Ecological Knowledge and Resource Management* (Philadelphia: Taylor & Francis, 1999).

14. Giovanna Di Chiro, "Response: Reengaging Environmental Education in the Anthropocene," *Australian Journal of Environmental Education* 30 (2014), 17.

15. See in this regard Adrienne Cachelin, Jeff Rose, and Dan Dustin, "Sustainability in Outdoor Education: Rethinking Root Metaphors," *Journal of Sustainability Education* 2 (2011).

to become responsible members of the wider human community and citizens of the biotic community. As Pope Francis writes: "There is a nobility in the duty to care for creation through little daily actions, and it is wonderful how education can bring about real changes in lifestyle" (211). Ecological education entails simple and concrete measures of caring for the natural world which is our common home.

> Education in environmental responsibility can encourage ways of acting which directly and significantly affect the world around us, such as avoiding the use of plastic and paper, reducing water consumption, separating refuse, cooking only what can reasonably be consumed, showing care for other living beings, using public transport or carpooling, planting trees, turning off unnecessary lights, or any number of other practices. (211)

Secondly, holistic ecological education should also lead to a greater sense of solidarity within the human family, especially with the more vulnerable members of our common household. To quote Pope Francis: "It [ecological education] needs educators capable of developing an ethics of ecology, and helping people, through effective pedagogy, to grow in solidarity, responsibility and compassionate care" (210).

The contemporary ecological crisis points not only to the unsustainable physical state of our planetary home but also of our common household. Education toward sustainability needs to inculcate precisely the virtues of kindness and solidarity in the young pupils if we are to construct a more equal and just world. The current educational scenario appears to be largely guided by the neoliberal agenda of free market which is taking its toll on human communities and ecosystems. Against such a situation we need to create a civilization of love and kindness, performing those small daily acts of solidarity, in a world where power and wealth tend to dominate and monopolize.[16] Solidarity can be a perfect antidote for neoliberal economic imperialism which is ravaging our home planet. Compassion and solidarity are indeed vital for the future of our planetary home and our common household.

Third, holistic ecological education "should facilitate making the leap towards the transcendent which gives ecological ethics its deepest meaning" (210), as Pope Francis points out in the encyclical. Education is complete only when it succeeds in inculcating a profound sense of the awareness of the presence of God in the natural world and in the lives of people.

The unsustainable situation of our common home, and of our common household, is ultimately caused by a profound rupture in our relationship with the Creator, the ground of all being, who has brought the entire material universe into existence and lovingly sustains it along with all forms of life. Humanity cannot expect to live in harmony with creation, if they are not at peace with the very Creator. Pope Benedict XVI offers a very poignant reflection in this regard:

> The brutal consumption of creation begins where God is missing, where matter has become simply material for us, where we ourselves are the ultimate measure, where everything is simply our property. . . . The waste of creation begins where we no longer recognize any claim beyond ourselves, seeing only ourselves.[17]

The ecological crisis arises precisely from our inability to perceive the physical world as God's creation, to respect its integrity, and to appreciate its intrinsic goodness and beauty, beyond mere considerations of utility and consumption.

16. See Pope Francis, Apostolic Exhortation *Evangelii Gaudium* (24 November 2013), 188.

17. Benedict XVI, *Meeting with Priests, Deacons, and Seminarians of the Diocese of Bolzano-Bressanone* (6 August 2008).

Education toward sustainability needs to be anchored in a profound religious sense of God's goodness and his loving presence in the natural world and in human history.

Laudato Si' points to the direction of ecological education today as reestablishing harmony with the natural world, fellow human beings, and the Creator. Such a holistic approach toward education is vital for the protection of our common planetary home in the context of the contemporary ecological crisis.

Settings for Ecological Education

In *Laudato Si'*, Pope Francis speaks of a variety of settings for ecological education: schools, families, media, catechesis, houses of religious formation. He insists on imparting such education right from an early age: "Good education plants seeds when we are young, and these continue to bear fruit throughout life" (213). Ecological education should cover the entire spectrum of our lives.

Pope Francis lays special emphasis on the role of the family in the arena of ecological education. The womb of the family is where one receives integral education. Here are some beautiful reflections from the pope in this regard:

> I would stress the great importance of the family, which is "the place in which life—the gift of God—can be properly welcomed and protected against the many attacks to which it is exposed, and can develop in accordance with what constitutes authentic human growth. In the face of the so-called culture of death, the family is the heart of the culture of life."[18] In the family we first learn how to show love and respect for life; we are taught the proper use of things, order and cleanliness, respect for the local ecosystem and care for

18. Pope John Paul II, Encyclical Letter *Centesimus Annus* (1 May 1991), 39: *AAS* 83 (1991), 842.

all creatures. In the family we receive an integral education, which enables us to grow harmoniously in personal maturity. In the family we learn to ask without demanding, to say "thank you" as an expression of genuine gratitude for what we have been given, to control our aggressivity and greed, and to ask forgiveness when we have caused harm. These simple gestures of heartfelt courtesy help to create a culture of shared life and respect for our surroundings. (213)

According to Pope Francis, "political institutions and various other social groups are also entrusted with helping to raise people's awareness" about the need to care for and protect our common planetary home. The pope proposes, given the importance of the question, that political institutions be "empowered to impose penalties for damage inflicted on the environment" (214). He is aware that these measures are not sufficient in themselves. Ultimately "we also need the personal qualities of self-control and willingness to learn from one another" (214).

Pope Francis points to the importance of educating toward the responsible stewardship of creation within the Catholic Church and in all Christian communities. According to Leonardo Franchi, *Laudato Si'* introduces a new term into the lexicon of Catholic education: "ecological education."[19] As the pope reminds us, "All Christian communities have an important role to play in ecological education" (214). Significantly, the pope makes explicit the paramount role of seminaries and houses of formation in ecological education, the very first papal statement ever to do so.[20] It needs to be acknowledged

---

19. Leonardo Franchi, "*Laudato Si'* and Ecological Education: Implications for Catholic Education," *Pensamiento Educativo: Journal of Latin American Educational Research* 53 (2016), 1.

20. See Yonatan Neril and Joy Auciello, *Report on Faith and Ecology Courses in North American Seminaries* (Jerusalem: The Interfaith Centre for Sustainable Development, 2015), 3.

that ecological questions do not receive the due attention in the formation of clergy and religious leaders around the world with detrimental consequences in their pastoral ministry when it comes to the question of the stewardship of creation. Against this background, Pope Francis writes in *Laudato Si'* in the context of ecological education:

> It is my hope that our seminaries and houses of formation will provide an education in responsible simplicity of life, in grateful contemplation of God's world, and in concern for the needs of the poor and the protection of the environment. (214)

Widening the scope of ecological education, Pope Francis speaks of the importance of aesthetic education, quoting Pope John Paul II: "The relationship between a good aesthetic education and the maintenance of a healthy environment cannot be overlooked"[21] (215). Pope Francis observes with keen insight: "If someone has not learned to stop and admire something beautiful, we should not be surprised if he or she treats everything as an object to be used and abused without scruple." He notes, "By learning to see and appreciate beauty, we learn to reject self-interested pragmatism" (215). We may recall in this regard the oft-quoted saying of Fyodor Dostoyevsky that "only beauty will save the world." We need to educate ourselves to appreciate the beauty of the natural world around us, if we are to save it for ourselves and for generations to come.

Pope Francis encourages us in the encyclical to make our small but precious contribution in the concrete settings of our lives toward the safeguarding of our common home. He writes in the context of ecological education:

> We must not think that these efforts are not going to change the world. They benefit society, often unbeknown to us,

21. John Paul II, *Message for the 1990 World Day of Peace*, 14: *AAS* 82 (1990), 155.

for they call forth a goodness which, albeit unseen, inevitably tends to spread. Furthermore, such actions can restore our sense of self-esteem; they can enable us to live more fully and to feel that life on earth is worthwhile. (212)

Importance of Education for Ecological Citizenship

The contemporary ecological crisis places humanity at crossroads with regard to its own future in our common home, Earth. The coming years will be crucial as we have precious little time left to pool together our resources and energies to protect and heal our common planetary home. Education toward sustainability is indeed one of the most urgent needs of our times. As Stephen Mulkey warns:

> It is likely that we have only about a decade to take sustainability seriously or we will lose the window of opportunity to salvage a livable planet for our children and grandchildren. Humanity faces a central choice: Live more sustainably on this planet, or face consequences that are incompatible with civilization. The choice really is that stark.[22]

The currently alarming state of our home planet is conspicuous evidence that we are far from living sustainably on Earth and that we have indeed a long way to go in this regard. At the same time, there are indeed several promising signs of hope in the arena of ecological education.

Significantly, one of the earliest responses to *Laudato Si'* was the signing of a statement on the part of leaders in Catholic higher education, including nearly a hundred university presidents from the United States alone, and others

22. Stephen Mulkey, "Sustainability Science as a Foundation for Higher Education in the Environmental Century," *Sustainability* 5/6 (2012), 356.

occupying significant posts in academic institutions around the world. *The Statement of Leaders in Catholic Higher Education Globally* praises the encyclical as a "timely, comprehensive, and inspiring" text and welcomes its "urgent call to action to address the climate and justice crises threatening the planet."

> Higher educational institutions globally must seek to provide influential leadership in discovering new and life-giving paths to address the pressing emergencies of climate change, social exclusion, and extreme poverty and in uncovering new paths to achieving peace, justice and environmental sustainability for the whole human family and the entire family of creation. . . .
>
> We commit ourselves as leaders in Catholic Higher Education to work together regionally and globally, through all the means available to and appropriate for our colleges and universities as institutions of higher learning, to study, promote, and act on the deals and vision of integral ecology laid out by Pope Francis.
>
> More specifically, we commit ourselves as leaders in Catholic Higher Education globally to integrate care for the planet, integral human development, and concern for the poor within our research projects, our educational curricula and public programming, our institutional infrastructures, policies and practices, and our political and social involvements as colleges and universities.[23]

It is heartening to realize that Pope Francis's call for ecological education in *Laudato Si'* is receiving such enthusiastic and high-level endorsements like the one we have just quoted

---

23. *Laudato Si': On Care for Our Common Home; Statement of Leaders in Catholic Higher Education Globally.* For the statement and list of signatories see: http://ignatiansolidarity.net/catholic-higher-ed-encyclical-sign-on/.

above. We cannot but anticipate more such responses from academic centers, churches and religions, and the wider civil society around the world in the area of ecological education. In the care of our increasingly imperiled common home, the role of education is indeed vital and indispensable.

GREEN COMMANDMENT IX
Embrace an Ecological Spirituality

In order to effect a radical change in our way of dwelling in our common home, Pope Francis proposes along with ecological education also an authentic creation spirituality. It is a spirituality that centers on respect and love for the totality of God's creation. The pope is aware that "Christians have not always appropriated and developed the spiritual treasures bestowed by God upon the Church, where the life of the spirit is not dissociated from the body or from nature or from worldly realities, but lived in and with them, in communion with all that surrounds us" (216). At the same time, he is convinced that "the rich heritage of Christian spirituality, the fruit of twenty centuries of personal and communal experience, has a precious contribution to make" (216) toward a creation spirituality for our times. In the encyclical, the pope offers suggestions for an ecological spirituality that can motivate and nourish our actions for the safeguarding of our common home:

> Here, I would like to offer Christians a few suggestions for an ecological spirituality grounded in the convictions of our faith, since the teachings of the Gospel have direct

consequences for our way of thinking, feeling and living. More than in ideas or concepts as such, I am interested in how such a spirituality can motivate us to a more passionate concern for the protection of our world. (216)

Our ninth green commandment is about the ecological spirituality of *Laudato Si'*. Following Pope Francis's lead in the encyclical, we outline the following contours of such a creation spirituality. It begins with a profound ecological conversion and entails sincere repentance for our sins against the Creator and the whole of creation. Creation spirituality is deeply incarnational as it finds expression in concrete attitudes and gestures of care and concern for our common home and the members of our common household. It also offers a sacramental vision of the natural world, leading us to perceive "God in all things." As Pope Francis points out in the encyclical, the whole of creation bears the trinitarian imprint, as it is ultimately God's handiwork, created and constantly sustained by God's infinite love. Creation has also a sublime eschatological destiny, namely, to be recapitulated in Christ in the fullness of time.

The Call to an Ecological Conversion

The crisis of our common home results from our sinful behavior, as we have seen earlier in the fourth green commandment. In *Laudato Si'*, Pope Francis talks about the root causes of the crisis and calls for a change of heart as their cure.[1] The ecological crisis thus becomes "a summons to profound interior conversion" (217). The encyclical "does not

---

1. Venugopalan Ittekkot and Eleanor Milne, "Encyclical Letter 'Laudato Si': A Gentle But Firm Nudge from Pope Francis," *Environmental Development* 17 (2016), 2.

so much ask for changes in terms of 'fixing problems,' but for changes in terms of 'converting the hearts.' "[2] We need today, what John Paul II called an "ecological conversion," if we are to manage to "finally stop before the abyss."[3] Pope Francis is also aware of the resistance to such an ecological conversion from some Christians:

> It must be said that some committed and prayerful Christians, with the excuse of realism and pragmatism, tend to ridicule expressions of concern for the environment. Others are passive; they choose not to change their habits and thus become inconsistent. So what they all need is an "ecological conversion," whereby the effects of their encounter with Jesus Christ become evident in their relationship with the world around them. (217)

The pope proposes the figure of St. Francis of Assisi as a model of ecological conversion "which entails the recognition of our errors, sins, faults and failures, and leads to heartfelt repentance and desire to change." He also recalls an invitation from the Australian bishops to achieve reconciliation with the whole of creation: "To achieve such reconciliation, we must examine our lives and acknowledge the ways in which we have harmed God's creation through our actions and our failure to act. We need to experience a conversion, or change of heart"[4] (218).

The needed "genuine conversion in ways of thought and behaviour,"[5] to use an expression of Pope John Paul II in his

2. Clemens Sedmark, "Traditional Concerns, New Language? Reflections on *Laudato Si'*," *The Heythrop Journal* 58 (2017), 949.

3. Pope John Paul II, General Audience Address (January 17, 2001).

4. Australian Catholic Bishops' Conference, *A New Earth—The Environmental Challenge* (2002).

5. John Paul II, *Peace with God the Creator, Peace with All of Creation*, n. 13.

1990 Message, is about learning to co-dwell in our common home of the Earth, with God the Creator, and with our fellow creatures, including humans. The ecological conversion is precisely about establishing peace with the Creator and the rest of creation.[6]

First of all, ecological conversion calls for a return to the Creator. The ecological crisis is, at the deepest level, "a rebellion against God as source and mystery of all created life, and our willful misuse of God's creation."[7] In this context, Seyyed Hossein Nasr had noted with great insight nearly half a century ago: "It is hopeless to expect to live in harmony with that grand theophany which is virgin nature, while remaining oblivious and indifferent to the Source of that theophany both beyond nature and at the centre of man's being."[8] In fact, faith traditions have always emphasized how in order to have peace and harmony with the natural world, one must be in harmony and equilibrium with heaven, and ultimately with the Source and Origin of all things.[9] Pope Benedict XVI speaks poignantly in this regard:

> Is it not true that an irresponsible use of creation begins precisely where God is marginalized or even denied? If the relationship between human creatures and the Creator is forgotten, matter is reduced to a selfish possession, man becomes the 'last word,' and the purpose of human exis-

6. See Joshtrom Isaac Kureethadam, *Creation in Crisis: Science, Ethics, Theology* (New York: Orbis, 2014), 359–62.

7. Frederick Quinn, *To Heal the Earth: A Theology of Ecology* (Nashville: Upper Room Books, 1994), 26.

8. Seyyed Hossein Nasr, *Man and Nature: The Spiritual Crisis of Modern Man* (Boston: Unwin, 1990), 9. The first edition of the book goes back to 1968.

9. See ibid., 136.

tence is reduced to a scramble for the maximum number of possessions possible.[10]

Just as the consequences of human sin falls on the land, apart from befalling the human community and their relationship with God, the repentance of the people of God will and can also lead to the healing of the land. It is a profound ecological truth that we find in the Sacred Scriptures. When people return to God and keep his covenant, then God will heal the land. As we read in the second book of the Chronicles: "If my people who are called by my name humble themselves, pray, seek my face, and turn from their wicked ways, then I will hear from heaven, and will forgive their sin and heal their land" (2 Chr 7:14). Dave Bookless writes in this regard:

> What is so significant is that healing the environment comes about not primarily by recycling, down-sizing or resource management, but by repentance and returning to God. The land can only be healed when its inhabitants recognize whose land it is, and repair their broken relationship with God and each other. If the ecological crisis is ultimately a spiritual crisis, then the cure is also a spiritual one.[11]

The conversion to the Creator in a humble and genuine spirit of repentance is fundamental if we are to heal our land and ourselves.

In second place, ecological conversion calls for a "turning" to the creation itself. In *Laudato Si'*, Pope Francis recalls the example of St. Francis of Assisi: "A healthy relationship with creation is one dimension of overall personal conversion" (218). For this, an ecological conversion is ultimately to the

10. Pope Benedict XVI, General Audience (26 August 2009).

11. Dave Bookless, *Planet Wise: Dare to Care for God's World* (Nottingham: Inter-Varsity Press, 2008), 58.

very Earth itself, the very *humus*, from where humans origi-
nated and whose stewardship was the primary task entrusted
to them. In the face of the crisis of our common home—as it
was in the aftermath of original sin of our first parents—the
Creator's command to humanity is to return to the earth and
to till the very ground from where they originally came.

> . . . until you return to the ground,
>   for out of it you were taken;
> you are dust,
>   and to dust you shall return. . . .
> [T]herefore the Lord God sent him forth from the garden
> of Eden, to till the ground from which he was taken.
> (Gen 3:19, 23)

A penitent return to the Earth is at the core of a genuine
ecological conversion. The salvation of the earth is intimately
tied to our humble return to it. Here is a very insightful passage from scripture scholar Brigitte Kahl:

> *Until you return to the earth. For from her you were taken.*
> Throughout the centuries, the "back to earth" of Gen. 3:19
> has been almost exclusively remembered at the tombs of
> the dead. Its challenge to Christian life practices was sel-
> dom heard. But the text very explicitly talks about a change
> of direction, for the Hebrew word for *return* implies also
> the theological dimension of repentance, turning back to
> God. Taking the fruit of the forbidden tree has damaged
> the relationship not only between God and Adam, but also
> between Adam and Adama, as the *thorns and thistles* dem-
> onstrate. When Adam is sent out from the garden, his task
> to serve the earth is repeated by God.[12]

12. Brigitte Kahl, "Fratricide and Ecocide: Rereading Genesis 2–4,"
in *Earth Habitat: Eco-Injustice and the Church's Response*, ed. Dieter Hessel
and Larry Rasmussen (Minneapolis: Fortress Press, 2001), 57.

Ecological conversion is above all at the personal level. In fact, at times a single person can make a decisive difference. Pope Francis recalls in this regard the edifying story of Noah in the Old Testament, whose personal righteousness saved not only himself and his kin from the destructive flood waters, but in a representative manner the rest of the biotic community. The pope writes: "Although 'the wickedness of man was great in the earth' (*Gen* 6:5) and the Lord 'was sorry that he had made man on the earth' (*Gen* 6:6), nonetheless, through Noah, who remained innocent and just, God decided to open a path of salvation. In this way he gave humanity the chance of a new beginning. All it takes is one good person to restore hope!" (71).

However, Pope Francis is quick to note that given the grave and global nature of the precarious situation of our common home individual efforts are not sufficient in themselves. A collective or communitarian ecological conversion is also equally important:

> Nevertheless, self-improvement on the part of individuals will not by itself remedy the extremely complex situation facing our world today. Isolated individuals can lose their ability and freedom to escape the utilitarian mindset, and end up prey to an unethical consumerism bereft of social or ecological awareness. Social problems must be addressed by community networks and not simply by the sum of individual good deeds. . . . The ecological conversion needed to bring about lasting change is also a community conversion. (219)

Pope Francis asks "all Christians to recognize and to live fully this dimension of their [ecological] conversion." He wishes and prays that "the power and the light of the grace we have received also be evident in our relationship to other creatures and to the world around us. In this way, we will help nurture that sublime fraternity with all creation which

Saint Francis of Assisi so radiantly embodied" (221). A true ecological conversion is thus at the heart of an authentic creation spirituality.

An Incarnational Spirituality

An authentic spirituality cannot but flow into life. It is all the more true in the case of an ecological spirituality, which is about learning to live responsibly and joyfully our existence in our common home. As the medieval mystic Hildegard of Bingen wrote, God created humankind so that we might "cultivate the earthly and thereby create the heavenly."[13]

Fundamental to ecological spirituality is the awareness of our profound communion with the rest of creation and our coresponsibility for our fellow creatures. Pope Francis writes:

> [Ecological spirituality] entails a loving awareness that we are not disconnected from the rest of creatures, but joined in a splendid universal communion. As believers, we do not look at the world from without but from within, conscious of the bonds with which the Father has linked us to all beings. . . . We do not understand our superiority as a reason for personal glory or irresponsible dominion, but rather as a different capacity which, in its turn, entails a serious responsibility stemming from our faith. (220)

Ecological spirituality is essentially an attitude of the heart, "one which approaches life with serene attentiveness, which is capable of being fully present to someone without thinking of what comes next, which accepts each moment as a gift from God to be lived to the full" (226). According to the pope, this was Jesus' own attitude:

13. *Meditations with Hildegard of Bingen*, ed. and trans. Gabriele Uhlein (Rochester, VT: Bear, 1983), 88.

Jesus taught us this attitude when he invited us to contemplate the lilies of the field and the birds of the air, or when seeing the rich young man and knowing his restlessness, "he looked at him with love" (*Mk* 10:21). He was completely present to everyone and to everything, and in this way he showed us the way to overcome that unhealthy anxiety which makes us superficial, aggressive and compulsive consumers. (226)

As Pope Francis points out in the encyclical, Christian spirituality proposes an alternative way of life and "encourages a prophetic and contemplative lifestyle one capable of deep enjoyment free of the obsession with consumption" (222). Such a lifestyle is particularly relevant in our era of ruthless consumerism which is slowly eroding our common home and its life-sustaining ecosystems. Christian spirituality is a real alternative in this regard. "It is a return to that simplicity which allows us to stop and appreciate the small things, to be grateful for the opportunities which life affords us, to be spiritually detached from what we possess, and not to succumb to sadness for what we lack" (222). An authentic creation spirituality manifests itself in a lifestyle of moderation.

Pope Francis states with great intuition that "no one can cultivate a sober and satisfying life without being at peace with him or herself" (225). Ecological spirituality for Pope Francis is also about cultivating a deeper inner peace within each one of us. "Inner peace is closely related to care for ecology and for the common good because, lived out authentically, it is reflected in a balanced lifestyle together with a capacity for wonder which takes us to a deeper understanding of life" (225). In a world of widespread restlessness and frenetic activity such a deeper inner peace alone can guarantee harmony with the rest of creation. The pope writes:

Nature is filled with words of love, but how can we listen to them amid constant noise, interminable and nerve-wracking distractions, or the cult of appearances? Many people today sense a profound imbalance which drives them to frenetic activity and makes them feel busy, in a constant hurry which in turn leads them to ride rough-shod over everything around them. This too affects how they treat the environment. An integral ecology includes taking time to recover a serene harmony with creation, reflecting on our lifestyle and our ideals, and contemplating the Creator who lives among us and surrounds us, whose presence "must not be contrived but found, uncovered."[14] (225)

Creation spirituality with its incarnational nature is to be lived out in space and time. We highlight in this regard two important institutions in our millennia long tradition, namely, the Jewish Sabbath and the Christian Sunday.

Pope Francis refers to the Sabbath in the encyclical. He recalls how the Sabbath came to be realized in the temporal order, spanning the rhythm of the days of the week, the cycle of seven years, and the great jubilee cycle of forty-nine years, as the institution of Sabbath went on to assume definite contours in the history of the people of God. As the pope notes, "This law came about as an attempt to ensure balance and fairness in their relationships with others and with the land on which they lived and worked" (71). The observance of the Sabbath assumed very concrete and down-to-earth implications in the Old Testament as evident in the Sabbath commandment given in the book of Exodus, where respect for Yahweh's sovereignty, care for the earth, concern for the poor, and sensitivity to the needs of both wild and farm animals are all intricately woven together.[15] As the pope writes, the

14. Pope Francis, Apostolic Exhortation *Evangelii Gaudium* (24 November 2013), 71: *AAS* 105 (2013), 1050.

15. See Seán McDonagh, *The Greening of the Church* (New York: Orbis, 1990), 127.

Sabbath was a clear "acknowledgment that the gift of the earth with its fruits belongs to everyone. Those who tilled and kept the land were obliged to share its fruits, especially with the poor, with widows, orphans and foreigners in their midst" (71). To celebrate Sabbath is to be at peace with fellow humans, especially the poor—the *anawim* of Yahweh—and with the whole of creation.

The Christian observance of Sunday as the Day of the Lord has profound ecological significance. Sunday is, above all, "the day of the Resurrection, the 'first day' of the new creation, whose first fruits are the Lord's risen humanity, the pledge of the final transfiguration of all created reality" (237). As Pope Francis indicates, "Sunday, like the Jewish Sabbath, is meant to be a day which heals our relationships with God, with ourselves, with others and with the world. . . . It also proclaims 'man's eternal rest in God' "[16] (237). The pope points to how the celebration of Sunday can truly incarnate ecological spirituality:

> Christian spirituality incorporates the value of relaxation and festivity. We tend to demean contemplative rest as something unproductive and unnecessary, but this is to do away with the very thing which is most important about work: its meaning. We are called to include in our work a dimension of receptivity and gratuity, which is quite different from mere inactivity. Rather, it is another way of working, which forms part of our very essence. It protects human action from becoming empty activism; it also prevents that unfettered greed and sense of isolation which make us seek personal gain to the detriment of all else. . . . Rest opens our eyes to the larger picture and gives us renewed sensitivity to the rights of others. And so the day of rest, centred on the Eucharist, sheds it light on the whole

16. *Catechism of the Catholic Church*, 2175.

week, and motivates us to greater concern for nature and
the poor. (237)

Spirituality, the pope notes, helps us to "recover a serene
harmony with creation, reflecting on our lifestyle and our
ideals, and contemplating the Creator who lives among us
and surrounds us" (225). It offers a sacramental vision of the
natural world as permeated by divine presence as we shall
go on to discuss now.

A Sacramental Vision of the Natural World

Ecological spirituality is profoundly sacramental as it helps
us "to discover God in all things," as Pope Francis affirms in
the encyclical. It is so since "the universe unfolds in God, who
fills it completely. Hence, there is a mystical meaning to be
found in a leaf, in a mountain trail, in a dewdrop, in a poor
person's face" (233). The pope quotes in this regard the Sufi
mystic Ali al-Khawas:

> The spiritual writer Ali al-Khawas stresses from his own
> experience the need not to put too much distance between
> the creatures of the world and the interior experience of
> God. As he puts it: "Prejudice should not have us criticize
> those who seek ecstasy in music or poetry. There is a subtle
> mystery in each of the movements and sounds of this
> world. The initiate will capture what is being said when
> the wind blows, the trees sway, water flows, flies buzz,
> doors creak, birds sing, or in the sound of strings or flutes,
> the sighs of the sick, the groans of the afflicted."[17] (233n159)

17. Eva De Vitray-Meyerovitch, ed., *Anthologie du soufisme* (Paris,
1978), 200.

Spirituality provides us, above all, with a different perception of the natural world, as imbued with divine presence. As Pope Francis points out, "Encountering God does not mean fleeing from this world or turning our back on nature" (235). The saints and mystics have been most attentive to the apparently veiled presence of God in the natural world. Pope Francis quotes in this regard Saint Bonaventure, who teaches us that "contemplation deepens the more we feel the working of God's grace within our hearts, and the better we learn to encounter God in creatures outside ourselves"[18] (233). The pope makes a particular mention of the great Catholic mystic Saint John of the Cross, who "taught that all the goodness present in the realities and experiences of this world 'is present in God eminently and infinitely, or more properly, in each of these sublime realities is God' "[19] (234). The pope goes on to clarify: "This is not because the finite things of this world are really divine, but because the mystic experiences the intimate connection between God and all beings, and thus feels that 'all things are God' "[20] (234). He quotes a beautiful passage from the writings of Saint John of the Cross in order to show how created things can indeed represent the Divine to us:

> "Mountains have heights and they are plentiful, vast, beautiful, graceful, bright and fragrant. These mountains are what my Beloved is to me. Lonely valleys are quiet, pleasant, cool, shady and flowing with fresh water; in the variety of their groves and in the sweet song of the birds, they afford abundant recreation and delight to the senses, and in their solitude and silence, they refresh us and give rest. These valleys are what my Beloved is to me."[21] (234)

18. Bonaventure, *In II Sent.*, 23, 2, 3.
19. John of the Cross, *Cántico Espiritual*, XIV, 5.
20. Ibid.
21. Ibid., XIV, 6–7.

The truth of the sacramental power of created realities to become means of communion with God is best expressed in the Christian praxis and theology of the sacraments, where fruits of the Earth can signify God's presence and become channels of God's presence and blessings. The sacramental life of the church draws deeply from the web of life.[22] Pope Francis writes, "The Sacraments are a privileged way in which nature is taken up by God to become a means of mediating supernatural life" (235). They thus become means of God's salvific action in time and space, here and now.

The archetype of all sacramental activity is Christ's Incarnation, of the Logos becoming flesh: of the intimate meeting and inextricable intertwining of the spiritual and the material.[23] For Hans Urs Von Balthasar, "The Incarnation expressed in a concentrated form the sacramental worldview of the Christian tradition in which creation is the very medium through which God is revealed."[24] Let us quote again from Pope Francis:

> For Christians, all the creatures of the material universe find their true meaning in the incarnate Word, for the Son of God has incorporated in his person part of the material world, planting in it a seed of definitive transformation. "Christianity does not reject matter. Rather, bodiliness is considered in all its value in the liturgical act, whereby the

22. See Sandra Yocum, "Liturgy: The Exaltation of Creation," in *The Theological and Ecological Vision of Laudato Si': Everything Is Connected*, ed. Vincent J. Miller (London: Bloomsbury, 2017), 127.

23. Philip Sherrard, *The Rape of Man and Nature: An Enquiry into the Origins and Consequences of Modern Science* (Suffolk: Golgonooza Press, 1987), 92.

24. Matthew T. Eggemeier, "A Sacramental Vision: Environmental Degradation and the Aesthetics of Creation," *Modern Theology* 29 (2013), 352.

human body is disclosed in its inner nature as a temple of
the Holy Spirit and is united with the Lord Jesus, who
himself took a body for the world's salvation."[25] (235)

It is on account of the mystery of the incarnation in which
God entered and embraced the whole of creation, and sanctified every created reality thereby, that "the Church does not
hesitate to bless and make generous use of the earth's materials in liturgical celebrations and sacraments."[26] Pope Francis
writes in this regard: "The hand that blesses is an instrument
of God's love and a reflection of the closeness of Jesus Christ,
who came to accompany us on the journey of life. Water
poured over the body of a child in Baptism is a sign of new
life." It is also true of other natural elements like oil, fire, and
colors which "are taken up in all their symbolic power and
incorporated in our act of praise" (235). The pope notes that
it is especially clear in the spirituality of the Christian East.
"Beauty, which in the East is one of the best loved names
expressing the divine harmony and the model of humanity
transfigured, appears everywhere: in the shape of a church,
in the sounds, in the colours, in the lights, in the scents"[27] (235).

Incarnational spirituality by which God is present to us
under the guise of material signs finds its apex in the Eucharist. As Pope Francis writes in the encyclical: "It is in the
Eucharist that all that has been created finds its greatest exaltation" (236). The pope offers us some profound reflections
on the mystery of the Eucharist:

25. John Paul II, Apostolic Letter *Orientale Lumen* (2 May 1995), 11:
AAS 87 (1995), 757.

26. Canadian Conference of Catholic Bishops, "You Love All That
Exists . . . All Things Are Yours, God, Lover of Life," A Pastoral Letter
on the Christian Ecological Imperative from the Social Affairs Commission (4 October 2003), 7.

27. John Paul II, *Orientale Lumen*, 11: *AAS*, 757.

Grace, which tends to manifest itself tangibly, found un-
surpassable expression when God himself became man
and gave himself as food for his creatures. The Lord, in the
culmination of the mystery of the Incarnation, chose to
reach our intimate depths through a fragment of matter.
He comes not from above, but from within, he comes that
we might find him in this world of ours. In the Eucharist,
fullness is already achieved; it is the living centre of the
universe, the overflowing core of love and of inexhaustible
life. (236)

When Christians gather for Eucharist, they bring the earth
and all its creatures, and in some way the whole universe, to
the altar.[28] The Eucharist is indeed an act of cosmic worship,
a sublime link between heaven and earth. Pope Francis writes:

Joined to the incarnate Son, present in the Eucharist, the
whole cosmos gives thanks to God. Indeed the Eucharist
is itself an act of cosmic love: "Yes, cosmic! Because even
when it is celebrated on the humble altar of a country
church, the Eucharist is always in some way celebrated on
the altar of the world."[29] The Eucharist joins heaven and
earth; it embraces and penetrates all creation. The world
which came forth from God's hands returns to him in
blessed and undivided adoration: in the bread of the Eucharist, "creation is projected towards divinization, towards the holy wedding feast, towards unification with
the Creator himself."[30] (236)

28. Denis Edwards, "Eucharist and Ecology," *SEDOS Bulletin* 41
(2009), 169.

29. John Paul II, Encyclical Letter *Ecclesia de Eucharistia* (17 April 2003),
8: *AAS* 95 (2003), 438.

30. Benedict XVI, *Homily for the Mass of Corpus Domini* (15 June 2006):
AAS 98 (2006), 513.

The Trinitarian Imprint and the Eschatological Destiny of All Creation

In *Laudato Si'*, Pope Francis describes how the trinitarian God is the origin, milieu, and destiny of the whole of creation and how each of the three Persons is intimately and uniquely present to the whole of creation:

> The Father is the ultimate source of everything, the loving and self-communicating foundation of all that exists. The Son, his reflection, through whom all things were created, united himself to this earth when he was formed in the womb of Mary. The Spirit, infinite bond of love, is intimately present at the very heart of the universe, inspiring and bringing new pathways. The world was created by the three Persons acting as a single divine principle, but each one of them performed this common work in accordance with his own personal property. (238)

According to Pope Francis, "for Christians, believing in one God who is trinitarian communion suggests that the Trinity has left its mark on all creation" (239). The pope refers to Saint Bonaventure in this regard:

> The reflection of the Trinity was there to be recognized in nature "when that book was open to man and our eyes had not yet become darkened."[31] The Franciscan saint teaches us that *each creature bears in itself a specifically Trinitarian structure*, so real that it could be readily contemplated if only the human gaze were not so partial, dark and fragile. In this way, he points out to us the challenge of trying to read reality in a Trinitarian key. (239)

31. Bonaventure, *Quaest. Disp. de Myst. Trinitatis*, 1, 2 concl.

The pope points out that "the divine Persons are subsistent relations" and our world is "a web of relationships" precisely since it is "created according to the divine model" (240). The trinitarian communion reflected in ecological interrelatedness in the created world also reveals our vocation to create bonds of unity and foster relationships. It is also the path for authentic human fulfillment. "The human person grows more, matures more and is sanctified more to the extent that he or she enters into relationships, going out from themselves to live in communion with God, with others and with all creatures" (240). Ecological spirituality which leads to global solidarity ultimately flows from the very mystery of the trinitarian communion. It is in this way that humans "make their own that trinitarian dynamism which God imprinted in them when they were created" (240).

Ecological spirituality is founded ultimately on the eschatological destiny of all creation to be recapitulated in Christ. God is the eschatological point of arrival of all creatures as Pope Francis writes in *Laudato Si'*: "All creatures are moving forward with us and through us towards a common point of arrival, which is God, in that transcendent fullness where the risen Christ embraces and illumines all things" (83). It is important to remember that it is the whole of creation, the entire physical universe, and not just humanity alone that is destined to be redeemed and transformed in Christ.[32] Pope Francis writes in the encyclical:

> At the end, we will find ourselves face to face with the infinite beauty of God (cf. 1 *Cor* 13:12), and be able to read with admiration and happiness the mystery of the universe, which with us will share in unending plenitude. Even now we are journeying towards the sabbath of eternity, the new

---

32. See Kureethadam, *Creation in Crisis*, 324–25.

Jerusalem, towards our common home in heaven. Jesus says: "I make all things new" (*Rev* 21:5). Eternal life will be a shared experience of awe, in which each creature, resplendently transfigured, will take its rightful place and have something to give those poor men and women who will have been liberated once and for all. (243)

The profound truth about the universal redemption of all things in Christ, which is the ultimate *telos* of all creation, places created goods in the eschatological light. The ecumenical patriarch Bartholomew I reminds us: "The final purpose of creation is not its use or abuse for humankind's individual pleasure, but something far more sublime and sacred."[33] Creation's true destiny is to be transformed and renewed in the risen Christ. Humanity's role, as Pope Francis indicates in the encyclical, is "to lead all creatures back to their Creator" (83).

33. Ecumenical Patriarch Bartholomew I, "Greeting during the Symposium at Holy Trinity Monastery, Halki, June 1, 1992," in *Cosmic Grace, Humble Prayer: The Ecological Vision of the Green Patriarch Bartholomew*, ed. John Chryssavgis (Grand Rapids, MI: Eerdmans, 2009), 84.

GREEN COMMANDMENT X
Cultivate Ecological Virtues

One of the significant contributions of *Laudato Si'* is Pope Francis's insistence on the cultivation of ecological virtues on the part of humanity for the responsible care of our common home. In the encyclical, the pope echoes the invitation from the Brazilian bishops for the cultivation of "ecological virtues"[1] (88). According to him, we will be able to protect and care for our common home only by learning to adopt radically new lifestyles, what he calls "new habits." Pope Francis is aware of how difficult it is to acquire such habits, especially in the context of widespread consumerism and cultural relativism as people "feel unable to give up what the market sets before them" (209). The pope is particularly aware of the challenges that young people face in this regard. They "have a new ecological sensitivity and a generous spirit, and some of them are making admirable efforts to protect the environment. At the same time, they have grown up in a milieu of extreme consumerism and affluence which makes it difficult to develop other habits" (209).

1. Cf. National Conference of the Bishops of Brazil, *A Igreja e a Questão Ecológica* (1992), 61.

The formation of healthy *habitus* for the stewardship of our common home can come only through the cultivation of appropriate "ecological virtues." Laws and regulations are insufficient in this regard and only the cultivation of sound ecological virtues can lead to a selfless ecological commitment:

> The existence of laws and regulations is insufficient in the long run to curb bad conduct, even when effective means of enforcement are present. If the laws are to bring about significant, long-lasting effects, the majority of the members of society must be adequately motivated to accept them, and personally transformed to respond. Only by cultivating sound virtues will people be able to make a selfless ecological commitment. (211)

The last of our green commandments is about the ecological virtues that we need to cultivate to become responsible stewards of our common home. The ecological virtues are not listed as such in the encyclical, but find repeated mention throughout the text. They are like signposts that indicate the road that we need to travel in caring for our common planetary home.

We shall now reflect at length on seven ecological virtues in *Laudato Si'*: praise, gratitude, care, justice, work, sobriety, and humility—virtues that will enable us to care in a more loving and responsible manner for our common planetary home.

Praise

The very title of the encyclical is an invitation to praise the Creator. *"Laudato Si' mi' Signore,"* "Praise be to you, my Lord," are the first lines of the Canticle of Creatures, which was composed by St. Francis of Assisi in the Umbrian dialect around 1225, the first vernacular Italian poem in history. Praise is a fundamental theme that runs throughout the encyclical and appears nearly thirty times in the text.

From a theological perspective, the very existence of creation, and of each and every creature, is to render glory and praise to God. Creation itself becomes an animate temple where the praise of God resounds.[2] The scriptures of various religious traditions, and the biblical tradition in particular, abound in references to the unceasing hymn of praise of created realities for the Creator. The Christian Scriptures are replete with references of creation's incessant liturgy of praise. As John Paul II reminded us in his 1990 Message, "The Bible speaks repeatedly of the goodness and beauty of creation, which is called to glorify God"[3] (cf. Gen 1:4ff.; Ps 8:2; 104:1ff.; Wis 13:3-5; Sir 39:16, 33; 43:1, 9).

The cosmic liturgy of praise is especially prevalent in the Psalms. The Psalms, as Pope Francis points out in *Laudato Si'*, "frequently exhort us to praise God the Creator, 'who spread out the earth on the waters, for his steadfast love endures for ever' (*Ps* 136:6). They also invite other creatures to join us in this praise: 'Praise him, sun and moon, praise him, all you shining stars! Praise him, you highest heavens, and you waters above the heavens! Let them praise the name of the Lord, for he commanded and they were created' (*Ps* 148:3-5)" (72). In fact, the last of the Psalms ends inviting "every living creature to praise the Lord" (*Ps* 150:6).

In the cosmic liturgy of praise, human beings, however, have a very special role. They are called not only to pray and sing along with all creation in the cosmic liturgy but also to become the very voice of creation's praise of the Creator.[4] It is the unique vocation of human beings to become the voice of the entire

---

2. See in this regard Edward Brown, *Our Father's World: Mobilizing the Church to Care for Creation* (South Hadley, MA: Doorlight Publications, 2006), 38–39.

3. Pope John Paul II, *Peace with God the Creator, Peace with All of Creation*. Message for the World Day of Peace (1 January 1990), 14.

4. See in this regard Daniel Castillo, " 'To Praise, Reverence and Serve': The Theological Anthropology of Pope Francis," in *The Theological and*

creation's unspoken worship of God. Leontius of Byzantium wrote in the ninth century: "The creation does not venerate the Maker directly and by itself, but it is through [us] that the heavens declare the glory of God, through [us] the moon worships God, through [us] the waters and showers of rain, the dew and all creation, venerate God and give glory to God."[5] Saint Francis of Assisi is a beautiful example in this regard. Pope Francis reminds us in the encyclical how Saint Francis broke out spontaneously into joyful praise before the beauty of creation:

> Just as happens when we fall in love with someone, whenever he would gaze at the sun, the moon or the smallest of animals, he burst into song, drawing all other creatures into his praise. He communed with all creation, even preaching to the flowers, inviting them "to praise the Lord, just as if they were endowed with reason."[6] His response to the world around him was so much more than intellectual appreciation or economic calculus, for to him each and every creature was a sister united to him by bonds of affection. (11)

We praise the Creator when we are able to recognize his very image reflected on the mirror of his creation. As the pope writes, "When we can see God reflected in all that exists, our hearts are moved to praise the Lord for all his creatures and to worship him in union with them" (87). It is such a sentiment that finds magnificent expression in Saint Francis of Assisi's "Canticle of Creatures." Pope Francis cites this beautiful and meticulously woven hymn of praise of the Creator for the wonders of his creation:

Ecological Vision of Laudato Si': Everything Is Connected, ed. Vincent J. Miller (London: Bloomsbury, 2017), 95–108.

5. Leontius of Byzantium, *Apologetic Sermon II on the Holy Icons*, in *Patrologia Graeca*, ed. J. Migne, 161 vols. (Paris, 1857–1928), 93:1604.

6. Thomas of Celano, *The Life of Saint Francis*, I, 29, 81, in *Francis of Assisi: Early Documents*, vol. 1 (New York: New City Press, 1999), 251.

Praised be you, my Lord, with all your creatures,
especially Sir Brother Sun,
who is the day
and through whom you give us light.
And he is beautiful and radiant
with great splendour;
and bears a likeness of you, Most High.
Praised be you, my Lord,
through Sister Moon and the stars,
in heaven you formed them clear
and precious and beautiful.
Praised be you, my Lord,
through Brother Wind,
and through the air, cloudy and serene,
and every kind of weather
through whom you give sustenance
to your creatures.
Praised be you, my Lord, through Sister Water,
who is very useful and humble
and precious and chaste.
Praised be you, my Lord, through Brother Fire,
through whom you light the night,
and he is beautiful and playful
and robust and strong."[7] (87)

Significantly, Pope Francis draws his encyclical to conclusion with a joyful invitation to join the chorus of creatures in a canticle of praise. "Let us sing as we go," he exhorts us (244).[8]

A fundamental problem of modern humans is their deafness to the cosmic symphony of praise that created realities continually raise to the Creator. We live in a world starved of wonder,

7. *Canticle of the Creatures*, in *Francis of Assisi*, 113–14.
8. See Elizabeth T. Groppe, " 'The Love that Moves the Sun and the Stars': A Theology of Creation," in *The Theological and Ecological Vision of Laudato Si': Everything Is Connected*, ed. Vincent J. Miller (London: Bloomsbury, 2017), 91.

which is the stepping-stone to praise. As Francis Schaeffer has written: "The wonder is all gone. Man sits in his autonomous 'decreated' world, where there are no universals and no wonder in nature. Indeed, ir. an arrogant and egoistic way, nature has been reduced to a 'thing' for man to use or exploit."[9]

Today, in the face of the crisis of our common home, we need to rediscover the sense of marvel and praise before the beauty of creation. As Pope Francis writes, "Rather than a problem to be solved, the world is a joyful mystery to be contemplated with gladness and praise" (12). In "the contemplation of beauty," as the pope notes, "a quantum leap occurs, resulting in a fulfilment which is uniquely human" (103). We will save our common home only when we learn to see it with a deep sense of wonder that wells up in spontaneous praise of the Creator for all the marvels of creation.

Gratitude

Closely linked with praise is the ecological virtue of gratitude. Pope Francis notes that unfortunately today nature is usually seen only "as a system which can be studied, understood and controlled, whereas creation can only be understood as a gift from the outstretched hand of the Father of all" (76). Gratitude springs up in our hearts when we accept "each moment as a gift from God to be lived to the full" (226). The foundation of a grateful existence on Earth is the profound realization "that the world is a gift which we have freely received and must share with others" (159). The pope repeats later in the encyclical that the "recognition that the world is God's loving gift" naturally "entails gratitude and gratuitousness" (220).

9. Francis A. Schaeffer, *Pollution and the Death of Man: The Christian View of Ecology* (Wheaton, IL: Tyndale House, 1970), 89.

A grateful outlook on the natural world has concrete implications in our dealing with created realities. As the pope writes: "Since the world has been given to us, we can no longer view reality in a purely utilitarian way, in which efficiency and productivity are entirely geared to our individual benefit" (159).

Pope Francis praises the indigenous communities for having preserved the original sense of gratitude for the gift of the land and of their bodies: "For them, land is not a commodity but rather a gift from God and from their ancestors who rest there, a sacred space with which they need to interact if they are to maintain their identity and values" (146).

Gratitude is a virtue we are fast losing today and Pope Francis invites us to recover it. He suggests we recover the simple habit of praying in thankfulness before and after meals:

> One expression of this attitude is when we stop and give thanks to God before and after meals. I ask all believers to return to this beautiful and meaningful custom. That moment of blessing, however brief, reminds us of our dependence on God for life; it strengthens our feeling of gratitude for the gifts of creation; it acknowledges those who by their labours provide us with these goods; and it reaffirms our solidarity with those in greatest need. (227)

The Eucharist is the greatest act of praise and gratitude that anyone can render to God. The verb *eucharisteo* in Greek means precisely to praise and to thank. In the Eucharist, the gift of creation, symbolized in the form of bread and wine, are lifted up in prayer and thanksgiving back to the very Creator. As the ecumenical patriarch Bartholomew writes:

> In the bread and wine of the Eucharist, as priests standing before the altar of the world, we offer the creation back to the Creator. . . . We celebrate the beauty of creation and consecrate the life of the world, returning it to God with thanks. . . . We offer the fullness of creation at the

> Eucharist, and receive it back as a blessing, as the living
> presence of God.[10]

Every Eucharist is a thanksgiving memorial, an anamnesis
of God's stupendous work in creation as well as in redemption. As Louis Bouyer has pointed out, the early Christian
eucharistic prayers, themselves modelled on Jewish prayer
forms used in synagogues and especially in homes and above
all in the Passover meal, always began with a blessing of the
gifts of creation, remembering and thanking God for his great
works in creation and in salvation.[11] The orthodox theologian
John Zizioulas, the Metropolitan of Pergamon, has shown
how all the ancient eucharistic liturgies began with thanksgiving for creation and then continued with thanksgiving for
redemption in Christ, and all of them were centered on the
lifting up of the gifts of creation to the Creator.[12]

The Eucharist is indeed a cosmic act of gratitude and worship. As Pope Francis writes in *Laudato Si'*: "Joined to the
incarnate Son, present in the Eucharist, the whole cosmos
gives thanks to God" (236). In this regard, Brandon Gallaher
points out: "The living symbol of a humble and grateful way
of life is the Eucharist. In the form of bread and wine, humanity offers back to God what is God's own and time and space
are sanctified."[13]

10. Ecumenical Patriarch Bartholomew I, "Address during the Environmental Symposium in Santa Barbara, November 8, 1997," in *Cosmic
Grace, Humble Prayer: The Ecological Vision of the Green Patriarch Bartholomew*, ed. John Chryssavgis (Grand Rapids, MI: Eerdmans, 2009), 188.

11. Louis Bouyer, *Life and Liturgy* (London: Sheed and Ward, 1956),
15–28.

12. John Zizioulas, "Preserving God's Creation," *King's Theological
Review* 12 (1989), 4.

13. Brandon Gallaher, "Common Themes for Our Common Home,"
The Tablet (4 July 2015), 13.

As priests of creation, human beings are also called to live the *eucharistic ethos*: "using the earth's natural resources with thankfulness, offering them back to God."[14] The gift (*doron*, in Greek) of creation, when offered back to the Creator in thanksgiving becomes a gift in return (*antidoron*, in Greek). "Nature is the *doron* of the Triune God to humankind. The *antidoron* of humankind to its Maker and Father is the respect of this gift, the preservation of creation, as well as its fruitful and careful use."[15] It also means sharing the gifts of creation generously with one's fellow brothers and sisters.

The crisis of our common home exposes our inability to lift up creation and created goods in praise and thanksgiving. Our abuse of creation and created goods ultimately reveals our ingratitude to the Creator. The ecological crisis exposes our incapacity to live the eucharistic ethos. We not only take the abundant gifts of creation for granted, but we also fail to share them with our fellow men and women, especially with the needy, in a spirit of communion (*koinonia*). We stand in need of living our lives gratefully on Earth, in the eucharistic way, giving thanks to God for the gift of creation and sharing it generously with others.

Care

Care is another important ecological virtue of *Laudato Si'*. In fact, the encyclical carries the subtitle *on "care" for our common home*. There is a subtle paradigm shift here from the

---

14. Bartholomew I, "Message for September 1, 1994," in *Cosmic Grace, Humble Prayer*, ed. Chryssavgis, 44.

15. Bartholomew I, "Toast during Chryssavgis the Banquet in Constanza, Second International Symposium, September 26, 1997," in *Cosmic Grace, Humble Prayer*, ed. Chryssavgis, 179–80.

oft- used "stewardship" language that has dominated Christian theology of creation for decades. In fact, the term stewardship, which often features heavily in faith-based calls for environmental concern, appears just twice in the entire encyclical. Pope Francis lays emphasis on care for creation rather than on stewardship. According to Cardinal Peter Turkson, care goes further than stewardship:

> Good stewards take responsibility and fulfil their obligations to manage and to render an account. But one can be a good steward without feeling connected. If one *cares*, however, one is connected. To *care* is to allow oneself to be affected by another, so much so that one's path and priorities change. Good parents know this. They care *about* their children; they care *for* their children, so much so that parents will sacrifice enormously—even their lives—to ensure the safety and flourishing of their children. With caring, the hard line between self and other softens, blurs, even disappears. Pope Francis proposes that we think of our relationship with the world and with all people in terms of *caring*.[16]

The pope states that the "ecological conversion" needed in the face of the crisis of our common home "calls for a number of attitudes which together foster a spirit of generous care, full of tenderness" (220). To care is authentically human and authentically Christian. As Jon M. Sweeney notes, "Care is an essential human capacity, a virtue requiring action," deeply rooted in the gospel Beatitudes and Christian humanism.[17] In caring for our common home and for the weaker

---

16. Peter K. A. Turkson, "Catholicism and the Environment: Reflections on *Laudato Si'*," International Conference for Catholic Bishops (Lisbon, 22 January 2016).

17. Jon M. Sweeney, "A Kinship of Harmony," *The Tablet* (20 June 2015), 4.

members of our common household, we are indeed imitating God's own loving, tender care toward all creatures. As Pope Francis writes in the encyclical, "Every creature is thus the object of the Father's tenderness, who gives it its place in the world" (77). We are called to "cooperate as instruments of God for the care of creation, each according to his or her own culture, experience, involvements and talents" (14).

Reflecting God in caring for creation is fundamental to what humans are. It is our clear job description in the Bible.[18] It is here, in fact, that humans reveal their specific identity of being created in the image of God (*imago Dei*). As Mark Bredin points out, "The essence of being made in the image of God is to care for creation as God cares and nourishes."[19] Fashioned in the image and likeness of God, the human being is expected to tend creation with the same care and compassion of God. As the former Archbishop of Canterbury, Rowen Williams, writes: "Genesis tells us that when we are called to relationship with our creator, we are in the same moment summoned to responsibility for the non-human world. That's how we express our relationship with the creator, our reality as made in God's image."[20]

An ethics of care is rooted in a specific view of the world as a network of relationships. Pope Francis writes that "we must regain the conviction that we need one another, that we have a shared responsibility for others and the world" (229). In fact, the basic "awareness of the connection between people gives rise to recognition of a responsibility for one

18. Dave Bookless, *Planet Wise: Dare to Care for God's World* (Nottingham: Inter-Varsity Press, 2008), 90.

19. Mark Bredin, "God the Carer: Revelation and the Environment," *Biblical Theology Bulletin* 38/2 (2008), 85.

20. Rowan Williams, "The Ark and the Covenant," *The Tablet* (24 October 2009), 10.

another."[21] The pope writes in the encyclical: "Disinterested concern for others, and the rejection of every form of self-centeredness and self-absorption, are essential if we truly wish to care for our brothers and sisters and for the natural environment" (208). He proposes some outstanding models from the Christian tradition in this regard. First among them is Saint Francis of Assisi:

> I believe that Saint Francis is the example par excellence of care for the vulnerable and of an integral ecology lived out joyfully and authentically. . . . He was particularly concerned for God's creation and for the poor and outcast. He loved, and was deeply loved for his joy, his generous self-giving, his openheartedness. He was a mystic and a pilgrim who lived in simplicity and in wonderful harmony with God, with others, with nature and with himself. He shows us just how inseparable the bond is between concern for nature, justice for the poor, commitment to society, and interior peace. (10)

According to Pope Francis, what really moved Saint Francis to care for all creatures was his realization of oneness with them: "For to him each and every creature was a sister united to him by bonds of affection. . . . His disciple Saint Bonaventure tells us that 'from a reflection on the primary source of all things, filled with even more abundant piety, he would call creatures, no matter how small, by the name of "brother" or "sister." '[22] Such a conviction cannot be written off as naive romanticism, for it affects the choices which determine our behaviour" (11). He goes on to write how a caring attitude is the natural outcome of such an approach:

21. Carol Gilligan, *In a Different Voice: Psychological Theory and Woman's Development* (Cambridge, MA: Harvard University Press, 1982), 30.
22. The Major Legend of Saint Francis, VIII, 6, in *Francis of Assisi: Early Documents*, vol. 2 (New York: New City Press, 2000), 590.

> If we approach nature and the environment without this
> openness to awe and wonder, if we no longer speak the lan-
> guage of fraternity and beauty in our relationship with the
> world, our attitude will be that of masters, consumers, ruth-
> less exploiters, unable to set limits on their immediate needs.
> By contrast, if we feel intimately united with all that exists,
> then sobriety and care will well up spontaneously. (11)

In the encyclical, Pope Francis proposes also other models
of care. Saint Therese of Lisieux, for example, "invites us to
practise the little way of love, not to miss out on a kind word,
a smile or any small gesture which sows peace and friendship" (230). The pope insists on such "little" steps to care for
our broken world. "An integral ecology is also made up of
simple daily gestures which break with the logic of violence,
exploitation and selfishness" (230).

Pope Francis speaks also of communitarian forms of care
that is "also civic and political, and it makes itself felt in every
action that seeks to build a better world" (231). Care can indeed create a civilization of love on Earth. For the pope, care
is nothing but the social expression of love or Christian char-
ity. He draws abundantly from Catholic social teachings:

> Love for society and commitment to the common good are
> outstanding expressions of a charity which affects not only
> relationships between individuals but also "macro-
> relationships, social, economic and political ones."[23] That
> is why the church set before the world the ideal of a "civi-
> lization of love."[24] Social love is the key to authentic devel-
> opment: "In order to make society more human, more
> worthy of the human person, love in social life—political,

23. Pope Benedict XVI, Encyclical Letter *Caritas in Veritate* (29 June
2009) 2: *AAS* 101 (2009), 642.
24. Pope Paul VI, *Message for the 1977 World Day of Peace*: *AAS* 68
(1976), 709.

economic and cultural—must be given renewed value, becoming the constant and highest norm for all activity."[25] In this framework, along with the importance of little everyday gestures, social love moves us to devise larger strategies to halt environmental degradation and to encourage a "culture of care" which permeates all of society. (231)

The perfect model of care is Mary, the Mother who cared for Jesus. She now "cares with maternal affection and pain for this wounded world. Just as her pierced heart mourned the death of Jesus, so now she grieves for the sufferings of the crucified poor and for the creatures of this world laid waste by human power" (241). Pope Francis mentions in this regard also Saint Joseph, who through his work and generous presence cared for and defended Mary and Jesus and who is also the custodian of the universal church. "He too can teach us how to show care; he can inspire us to work with generosity and tenderness in protecting this world which God has entrusted to us" (242).

Justice

Justice becomes an important ecological virtue in the context of the great inequalities that coexist with and largely contribute to the crisis of our common home. In fact, today we need to speak of "eco-justice." The foundation for eco-justice is the common destination of all material goods, namely, that created goods belong to all. Pope Francis writes:

Whether believers or not, we are agreed today that the earth is essentially a shared inheritance, whose fruits are meant to benefit everyone. For believers, this becomes a

25. Pontifical Council for Justice and Peace, *Compendium of the Social Doctrine of the Church*, 582.

question of fidelity to the Creator, since God created the world for everyone. Hence every ecological approach needs to incorporate a social perspective which takes into account the fundamental rights of the poor and the under-privileged. (93)

However, though "the natural environment is a collective good, the patrimony of all humanity, . . . twenty percent of the world's population consumes resources at a rate that robs the poor nations and future generations of what they need to survive"[26] (95). According to the pope, "This vision of 'might is right' has engendered immense inequality, injustice, and acts of violence against the majority of humanity since resources end up in the hands of the first comer or the most powerful: the winner takes all" (82). The pope does not hesitate to point out that such a situation is "completely at odds" with "the ideals of harmony, justice, fraternity and peace as proposed by Jesus" (82).

The contemporary ecological crisis becomes an epitome of injustice on account of the tragic truth that is caused largely by the rich and affluent, but its disproportionate victims are the poor and vulnerable.[27] While the ecological crisis affects our common home and its common household, its deleterious impacts fall mainly on the poor and the most vulnerable sections of our society. The ecological crisis is brewed within the crucible of inequality. The injustices brewed by the contemporary ecological crisis are conspicuously manifest in the case of climate change, the greatest of the ecological challenges facing humanity. There is no dearth of assessments which emphasize the fact that the impacts of climate change are falling first and most heavily on the "poorest and most

26. New Zealand Catholic Bishops Conference, *Statement on Environmental Issues* (1 September 2006).

27. See Joshtrom Isaac Kureethadam, *Creation in Crisis: Science, Ethics, Theology* (New York: Orbis, 2014), 254–57.

vulnerable people around the world."[28] We quote Chris J. Cuomo in this regard:

> Climate change was manufactured in a crucible of inequality, for it is a product of the industrial and the fossil-fuel eras, historical forces powered by exploitation, colonialism, and nearly limitless instrumental use of 'nature.' The world's wealthiest nations, and the privileged elite and industry-owning sectors of nearly all nations, have built fortunes and long-term economic stability on decades of unchecked development and energy consumption. By dumping harmful waste into the common atmosphere we have endangered everyone, including those who have contributed little or nothing at all to the industrial greenhouse effect: the 'least developed' nations, the natural world, and future generations.[29]

Robert Henson expresses well the tragic irony of an ecological problem like climate change that will affect the poor most, yet they have contributed least to its underlying causes:

> If all that global warming did was to make life a bit steamier for the people who consume the most fossil fuels, then there'd be a karmic neatness to it. Alas, climate change doesn't keep its multitude of effects so nicely focused. A warming planet is liable to produce a cascade of repercussions for millions of people who have never started up a car or taken a cross-country flight.[30]

The contemporary ecological crisis reveals a profound situation of injustice in which the lifestyles of the minority

28. Chris J. Cuomo, "Climate Change, Vulnerability, and Responsibility," *Hypatia* 26 (2011), 693.

29. Ibid.

30. Robert Henson, *The Rough Guide to Climate Change* (London: Rough Guides, 2006), 139.

affluent societies are threatening the very livelihoods of the more vulnerable populations of our common household. Justice demands paying back debts incurred. As *Caritas Internationalis* points out, the developed world has borrowed from the development potential of poorer countries and these "loans" must be repaid.[31] In the context of the crisis of our common home what we need today is not so much philanthropy but justice for the poor. Pope Francis writes in the encyclical, citing Pope Benedict, "Only when 'the economic and social costs of using up shared environmental resources are recognized with transparency and fully borne by those who incur them, not by other peoples or future generations,'[32] can those actions be considered ethical" (195).

The contemporary ecological crisis is ultimately about justice. It is about justice between communities of the same generation (intragenerational) and between current and future generations (intergenerational). As Pope Francis asserts in *Laudato Si'*, "We can be silent witnesses to terrible injustices if we think that we can obtain significant benefits by making the rest of humanity, present and future, pay the extremely high costs of environmental deterioration" (36).

Eco-justice is primarily about concern for the poor and vulnerable members of our common household, "whose life on this earth is brief and who cannot keep on waiting" (162). Hence, there is "an urgent moral need for a renewed sense of intragenerational solidarity"[33] (162). Eco-justice demands that the right to development of the poor and the question of poverty alleviation be placed at the heart of a true moral response to the crisis of our common home. Again Pope Francis writes,

31. Caritas Internationalis, *Climate Justice: Seeking a Global Ethic* (2009), 4.

32. Benedict XVI, *Caritas in Veritate*, 50: *AAS*, 686.

33. Benedict XVI, *Message for the 2010 World Day of Peace*, 8: *AAS* 102 (2010), 45.

"We need to reflect on our accountability before those who will have to endure the dire consequences" (161).

Eco-justice is also intergenerational. According to Pope Francis, "our inability to think seriously about future generations is linked to our inability to broaden the scope of our present interests and to give consideration to those who remain excluded from development" (162). Intergenerational solidarity is ultimately a question of justice:

> Intergenerational solidarity is not optional, but rather a basic question of justice, since the world we have received also belongs to those who will follow us. The Portuguese bishops have called upon us to acknowledge this obligation of justice: "The environment is part of a logic of receptivity. It is on loan to each generation, which must then hand it on to the next."[34] (159)

The care for our imperiled common home requires that we become passionate agents of eco-justice. As Pope Francis notes, the faith that sustains us in our struggle for justice is that the "God who created the universe out of nothing can also intervene in this world and overcome every form of evil. Injustice is not invincible" (74).

Work

The down-to-earth character of *Laudato Si'* is most evident in the ecological virtue of work. "Any approach to an integral ecology, which by definition does not exclude human beings, needs to take account of the value of labour, as Saint John Paul II wisely noted in his Encyclical *Laborem Exercens*" (124).

---

34. Portuguese Bishops' Conference, Pastoral Letter *Responsabilidade Solidária pelo Bem Comum* (15 September 2003), 20.

Significantly, Pope Francis dedicates a number of paragraphs in the encyclical to the theme of work and the dignity of human labor.

In the overall context of caring for our common home in peril, Pope Francis understands human work to be collaborating with God's handiwork of creation:

> According to the biblical account of creation, God placed man and woman in the garden he had created (cf. *Gen* 2:15) not only to preserve it ("keep") but also to make it fruitful ("till"). Labourers and craftsmen thus "maintain the fabric of the world" (*Sir* 38:34). Developing the created world in a prudent way is the best way of caring for it, as this means that we ourselves become the instrument used by God to bring out the potential which he himself inscribed in things. (124)

We read in the creation narratives that the stewardship of creation is the first and primary task entrusted to Adam, the first human being.[35] It is the very first commandment given to humanity. An important characteristic of the theme of stewardship in the book of Genesis is that humans are called to be co-carers of creation along with God. God is already caring for his creation. Humans need only to assist him, to partake of God's stewardship of the world. As the ecumenical patriarch Bartholomew I reminds us: "God has not allowed humanity to be a mere *spectator* or an irresponsible *consumer* of the world and of all that is in the world. Indeed, humanity has been called to assume the task of being primarily a *partaker* and a *sharer in the responsibility* for everything in the created world."[36] Here human work finds its noblest ideal as partaking in God's own work to maintain our common home.

35. See Kureethadam, *Creation in Crisis*, 329–31.
36. Bartholomew I, "Message for September 1, 1992," in *Cosmic Grace, Humble Prayer*, ed. Chryssavgis, 39.

In *Laudato Si'*, Pope Francis speaks of how Jesus worked with his hands and notes how most of his life was spent in ordinary work. Jesus thus sanctified human labor and our humble efforts to be good stewards to all of God's creation. We quote a beautiful paragraph from the encyclical here:

> Jesus worked with his hands, in daily contact with the matter created by God, to which he gave form by his crafts-manship. It is striking that most of his life was dedicated to this task in a simple life which awakened no admiration at all: "Is not this the carpenter, the son of Mary?" (*Mk* 6:3). In this way he sanctified human labour and endowed it with a special significance for our development. (98)

Pope Francis points out how the Christian tradition has "developed a rich and balanced understanding of the mean-ing of work" and cites also recent examples like Blessed Charles de Foucauld (125). The pope makes a special refer-ence to the millennia-long Christian monastic tradition. The monastic spiritual intuition concerning work is particularly relevant today in the care of our common home:

> We can also look to the great tradition of monasticism. Originally, it was a kind of flight from the world, an escape from the decadence of the cities. The monks sought the desert, convinced that it was the best place for encounter-ing the presence of God. Later, Saint Benedict of Norcia proposed that his monks live in community, combining prayer and spiritual reading with manual labour (*ora et labora*). Seeing manual labour as spiritually meaningful proved revolutionary. Personal growth and sanctification came to be sought in the interplay of recollection and work. This way of experiencing work makes us more protective and respectful of the environment; it imbues our relation-ship to the world with a healthy sobriety. (126)

Pope Francis offers some profound reflections on human labor in the encyclical, noting that a proper relationship between human beings and the natural world around us requires "a correct understanding of work." He proposes a rather holistic understanding of work: "This has to do not only with manual or agricultural labour but with any activity involving a modification of existing reality, from producing a social report to the design of a technological development" (125). Further on he states that "work is a necessity, part of the meaning of life on this earth, a path to growth, human development and personal fulfilment" (128). Work is the noble sphere for the personal growth of all human beings and their relationships at all levels:

> We need to remember that men and women have "the capacity to improve their lot, to further their moral growth and to develop their spiritual endowments."[37] Work should be the setting for this rich personal growth, where many aspects of life enter into play: creativity, planning for the future, developing our talents, living out our values, relating to others, giving glory to God. (127)

According to the pope, "we were created with a vocation to work." Therefore, "the goal should not be that technological progress increasingly replace human work, for this would be detrimental to humanity." It is important, then, to guarantee people, especially on the part of those in authority, "a dignified life through work" (128). The pope is critical of the current economic systems which often do not recognize the dignity of human labor and generate high rates of unemployment as they are more concerned about technological progress and accumulation of capital:

37. Paul VI, Encyclical Letter *Populorum Progressio* (26 March 1967), 34: *AAS* 59 (1967), 274.

Yet the orientation of the economy has favoured a kind of technological progress in which the costs of production are reduced by laying off workers and replacing them with machines. This is yet another way in which we can end up working against ourselves. The loss of jobs also has a negative impact on the economy "through the progressive erosion of social capital: the network of relationships of trust, dependability, and respect for rules, all of which are indispensable for any form of civil coexistence."[38] (128)

Laudato Si' has been hailed as an ecological and social encyclical at the same time. Pope Francis's profound reflections on the dignity of human labor as a means to care for our common home and for the members of our common household certainly appear to support such a claim.

Sobriety

Today our common home is crumbling because of unbridled consumption on the part of the rich minority. It is not the mass of poor people that destroys the planet, but the consumption of the rich. In fact, we live in a very ironical situation today with the rich overconsuming and the poor struggling to make ends meet. Pope Francis states forthrightly in this regard: "We fail to see that some are mired in desperate and degrading poverty, with no way out, while others have not the faintest idea of what to do with their possessions, vainly showing off their supposed superiority and leaving behind them so much waste which, if it were the case everywhere, would destroy the planet" (90).

When our planetary home is on the brink of collapse because of overconsumption of the natural resources, it is im-

---

38. Benedict XVI, *Caritas in Veritate*, 32: *AAS*, 666.

portant to rediscover sobriety in our lifestyles. Pope Francis therefore calls for a "bold cultural revolution" of sobriety in our times. The crisis of our common home demands that humanity effect a radical transition from affluence and wasteful abundance to sufficiency and moderation.[39] An ecologically sustainable lifestyle calls for a certain degree of asceticism, the sure antidote for the ills of our consumerist society. It is a virtue totally eclipsed in our consumerist culture, which we need to rediscover, if we are to save our planetary home and defend the vulnerable members of our common human family. The pope states that it is when we are willing to be ascetic that we can truly offer ourselves to God "as a living sacrifice, holy and acceptable (*Rom* 12:1)" (220).

The Eastern Christian tradition is rich in the theology of asceticism. Pope Francis therefore rightly invites us to heed the ecological teaching of the ecumenical patriarch Bartholomew I in this regard:

> He asks us to replace consumption with sacrifice, greed with generosity, wastefulness with a spirit of sharing, an asceticism which "entails learning to give, and not simply to give up. It is a way of loving, of moving gradually away from what I want to what God's world needs. It is liberation from fear, greed and compulsion."[40] (9)

Any radical and long-standing solution to the crisis of our common home presupposes our willingness to alter extravagant lifestyles. It is not an easy task. But there is no alternative. According to the ecumenical patriarch, "a reduction of

39. On the concept of sufficiency as against overconsumption, see Hélène Gorge et al., "What Do We Really Need? Questioning Consumption Through Sufficiency," *Journal of Macromarketing* 35 (2015), 11–22.

40. Bartholomew I, *Lecture at the Monastery of Utstein*, Norway (23 June 2003).

human consumption and the embrace of a life of simplicity are needed so that resources are preserved for future generations and the poorest."[41] We have no common future unless we save our planet and are willing to share its resources with our poorer brothers and sisters through a lifestyle of ecological sustainability. We recall in this regard the prophetic admonition of Pope John Paul II in the aforementioned 1990 Message:

> Modern society will find no solution to the ecological problem unless it *takes a serious look at its lifestyle*. In many parts of the world society is given to instant gratification and consumerism while remaining indifferent to the damage which these cause. . . . Simplicity, moderation and discipline, as well as a spirit of sacrifice, must become a part of everyday life, lest all suffer the negative consequences of the careless habits of a few.[42]

Pope Francis asks for limits to be put on growth, or even for decreased growth in the rich and developed world, going against the current myth of infinite economic growth: "The time has come to accept decreased growth in some parts of the world, in order to provide resources for other places to experience healthy growth" (193).

The invitation to tread gently on Earth through the adoption of a sober and simple lifestyle is at the core of Christian spirituality. Pope Francis writes in this regard:

> Christian spirituality proposes an alternative understanding of the quality of life, and encourages a prophetic and contemplative lifestyle, one capable of deep enjoyment

41. Ibid.
42. Pope John Paul II, *Peace with God the Creator, Peace with All of Creation*, no. 13.

free of the obsession with consumption. We need to take
up an ancient lesson, found in different religious traditions
and also in the Bible. It is the conviction that "less is more."
A constant flood of new consumer goods can baffle the
heart and prevent us from cherishing each thing and each
moment. To be serenely present to each reality, however
small it may be, opens us to much greater horizons of
understanding and personal fulfilment. (222)

As Pope Francis points out, "Such sobriety, when lived
freely and consciously, is liberating. It is not a lesser life or one
lived with less intensity. On the contrary, it is a way of living
life to the full. . . . Happiness means knowing how to limit
some needs which only diminish us, and being open to the
many different possibilities which life can offer" (223). Sobriety,
notes Pope Francis, is to see the world with the eyes of God
and from the vantage point of the poor. He told the Roman
Curia officials in his 2015 customary Christmas address:

> Sobriety . . . is the ability to renounce what is superfluous
> and to resist the dominant consumerist mentality. Sobriety
> is prudence, simplicity, straightforwardness, balance and
> temperance. Sobriety is seeing the world through God's
> eyes and from the side of the poor. Sobriety is a style of life
> which points to the primacy of others as a hierarchical
> principle and is shown in a life of concern and service
> toward others. The sober person is consistent and straight-
> forward in all things, because he or she can reduce, recover,
> recycle, repair, and live a life of moderation.[43]

Today, in the context of the crisis of our common home,
we need to challenge our current mind-set and our profligate

43. Pope Francis, *Presentation of the Christmas Greetings to the Roman Curia* (21 December 2015), no. 12.

consumerist lifestyles, if we are to save our home planet for ourselves and for future generations. It is time to recover the wise traditions of humanity that greatly value the virtues of sufficiency, moderation, and contentment. The freedom from avarice and the joy of simplicity are essential dicta of almost all the faiths.[44] It is in returning to a simple lifestyle that we return to the lap of mother Earth, who has sufficient for everyone's need but not for everyone's greed, as Mahatma Gandhi used to say. Gandhi's plea to "live simply so that others may simply live" is the pope's ultimate admonition in *Laudato Si'*.[45] Only a lifestyle of sobriety can save our common planetary home wrecked by our reckless consumerist lifestyles.

Humility

Humility is the mother of all ecological virtues. Pope Francis notes that "sobriety and humility were not favourably regarded in the last century. And yet, when there is a general breakdown in the exercise of a certain virtue in personal and social life, it ends up causing a number of imbalances, including environmental ones" (224). According to Pope Francis, lack of humility leads to mindless domination over the planet:

> Once we lose our humility, and become enthralled with the possibility of limitless mastery over everything, we inevitably end up harming society and the environment. It is not easy to promote this kind of healthy humility or happy sobriety when we consider our selves autonomous,

44. Tim O'Riordan et al., "The Legacy of the Papal Encyclical," *Environment: Science and Policy for Sustainable Development* 57/6 (2015), 3.

45. Susan Jacobson, Bill Weis, and Abigail B. Schneider, "*Laudato Si'* and the Consumption Challenge: Giving Students a Visceral Exercise in Saving Our Planet," *Jesuit Higher Education: A Journal* 6 (2017), 87.

> when we exclude God from our lives or replace him with
> our own ego, and think that our subjective feelings can
> define what is right and what is wrong. (224)

The contemporary ecological crisis stems ultimately from our refusal to recognize our humble self-identity as creatures. It is the sin of human *hubris* which lies, in fact, at the root of our irresponsible stewardship of God's creation and of our common household. As Michael S. Northcott rightly notes, the crisis of our common home results ultimately from our refusal to see ourselves as creatures. "At the heart of the pathology of ecological crisis is the refusal of modern humans to see themselves as creatures, contingently embedded in networks of relationships with other creatures, and with the Creator."[46]

The ecological crisis results from our negation of our radical dependence on the Creator, and the "refusal to accept limits placed upon humanity on account of its creaturely status."[47] Our current ecological predicament results from our stubborn refusal to accept any limit whatsoever—be it regarding the carrying capacity of the Earth in the case of the "ecological footprint" of individuals, communities, and nations, or in the case of the "carbon footprint" directly linked to climate change, as we have seen earlier. At a deeper level, such a refusal is a rebellion against the very natural order of creation conferred on it by God and a revolt ultimately against the very Creator. In fact, the refusal to accept any limit that arises from our creaturely status was the original sin of humanity, as we read in the third chapter of the book of Genesis. Such an arrogant posturing also masks the unbridled human

46. Michael S. Northcott, *A Moral Climate: The Ethics of Global Warming* (London: D.L.T.—Christian Aid, 2007), 14. See also pp. 5 and 16.

47. Alister McGrath, *The Reenchantment of Nature: The Denial of Religion and the Ecological Crisis* (New York: Doubleday, 2002), 79.

desire to have dominion over all of creation, overruling God's exclusive lordship over his creation.

The classical Greeks described *hubris* precisely as "the desire to become greater than the gods" (Euripides). The human defiance of God's lordship over creation and the human urge to usurp the power and privileges of the Creator are also evident in the narrative about the building of the Tower of Babel (Gen 11:1ff.). As Alister McGrath points out: "It is a powerful symbol of the human refusal to accept limits— whether natural or ordained—and to quest for domination and transformation. It is in the birth of this mind-set that the true roots of our ecological crisis lie."[48] Our kingly role over creation, conferred on us in total gratuity in spite of our absolute insignificance—as poignantly expressed in Psalm 8— cannot be exercised "on our own but only in dependence on our Lord, the Creator, Sustainer, Saviour God."[49] We are *imago Dei* and not our own images. Pope Benedict XVI writes in this regard: "The first step toward a correct relationship with the world around us is the recognition by humans of their status as created beings. Man is not God; he is His image."[50] According to Anna Rowlands, one of the central insights of *Laudato Si'* is that "the root of the ecological crisis lies in the failure to accept the idea of limits, and the truth of a Creator-creature relation."[51]

The crisis of our common home reveals how we have denied our creaturely identity as *imago mundi*—created like every other creature from the dust of the earth, from *humus*, the etymological root of the term humility. Today we need to

---

48. Ibid.

49. Dave Bookless, *Planet Wise: Dare to Care for God's World* (Nottingham: Inter-Varsity Press, 2008), 95.

50. Benedict XVI, General Audience (9 March 2011).

51. Anna Rowlands, "*Laudato Si'*: Rethinking Politics" (Guest Editorial), *Political Theology* 16/5 (2015), 418.

rediscover our self-identity as *imago mundi*, created from the dust of the earth. Our creaturely identity as *imago mundi* and our intimate fellowship and consequent interdependence with the rest of creation is clearly evident in the first pages of the Bible, especially in the older Yahwist narrative of creation. For the Yahwist author, human life and identity emerge out of arable soil. The very name Adam is from the Hebrew *adamah*, meaning literally "earth" or "soil." So we are basically "earthlings," we are creatures of the earth, with feet of clay.[52] An awareness of this earthly origin should enable us to regain an authentic sense of humility before the Creator and the rest of the created world. Significantly, *humilitas*, the Latin word for humility, literally means to be "grounded." Such creaturely humility will indeed be a sure antidote for the *hubris* of modern anthropocentrism in which lie some of the main roots of the crisis of our common home.

Pope Francis refers in the encyclical to Saint Joseph as a just man, hard-working and strong but showing also great tenderness. The pope then goes on to point out with insight that tenderness is "not a mark of the weak but of those who are genuinely strong," of those who are "fully aware of reality and ready to love and serve in humility" (242). Our imperiled common home requires committed persons willing to serve in humility. Ecological humility is indeed vital for the salvation of Earth and of humanity today. As one of the gospel beatitudes states: "Blessed are the meek, for they will inherit the earth" (Matt 5:5).

52. Bookless, *Planet Wise*, 31–32.

Conclusion

"The Zeal for Your House Shall Inflame Me"

In the second chapter of the Gospel of John, there is a verse that the disciples attribute to Jesus as he drives out money lenders and sellers of sheep and cattle from the temple of Jerusalem: "Zeal for your house will consume me" (v. 17). Prior to that verse Jesus tells those who are despoiling the holy place: "Stop making my Father's house a marketplace!" (v. 16).

In the above gospel passage, there are different levels of interpretation regarding the "house" about which Jesus was aflame with zeal. The Jews understood it as the temple. The disciples, after Jesus' own resurrection, understood it as his body. Today, we could, and probably we should, understand this house as our common planetary home. It is this common home which is being despoiled and desecrated today.

Significantly, our common home is also God's own house, permeated by the Spirit of God from the dawn of creation, where the Son of God pitched his tent in the supreme event of the incarnation. It is in this common home that God co-dwells with humanity and of which we have been entrusted with stewardship, as we read in the book of Genesis. The contemporary ecological crisis, in fact, lays bare precisely our incapacity to perceive the physical world as impregnated with divine presence. We have swapped the lofty vision of the physical world as God's own abode, sanctified by the incarnation of the Son of God, with the one-dimensional mechanistic outlook of modernity. Accordingly, the physical world gets reduced to a mere storehouse of resources for human consumption, just real estate for market speculation. It is such a reductive perception of the physical world which has enabled both materialistic and neoliberal economic systems, aided by modern technology, to ravage our home planet. Through pollution of the planet's land, air, and waters, we have degraded our common home that is also God's own home. We have turned this sacred abode into a marketplace.

In a situation of planetary emergency like the collapse of our planetary abode, we need to be aflame once again with the zeal for our common home.

Pope Francis's encyclical letter *Laudato Si'* is precisely about becoming aflame with the zeal to care for our common home. It is a huge responsibility that we owe especially to the more vulnerable members of our common household, who are the early and disproportionate victims of the degradation of our common home. We owe it also to the future generations. One of the most powerful questions raised by Pope Francis in the encyclical and which resounds loudly in our ears, even after we have laid down the text, is: "What kind of world do we want to leave to those who come after us, to children who are now growing up?" The pope goes on to warn us: "Leaving an inhabitable planet to future generations is, first and foremost, up to us. The issue is one which dramatically affects us, for it has to do with the ultimate meaning of our earthly sojourn" (160).

The contemporary ecological crisis which places in jeopardy the very habitability of our common planetary home is certainly the greatest of challenges that humanity has ever faced. We are aware today of the gravity of the crisis, thanks to the contribution from "numerous scientists, philosophers, theologians and civic groups" as Pope Francis himself acknowledges in the encyclical (7). History will judge *Laudato Si'* also as having made an important contribution in this regard.

The silver lining in the clouds is that our awareness of the crisis of our common home can become an opportunity to care for it more responsibly and build a more just and fraternal common household. As Pope Francis writes, "Although the post-industrial period may well be remembered as one of the most irresponsible in history, nonetheless there is reason to hope that humanity at the dawn of the twenty-first century will be remembered for having generously shouldered its grave responsibilities" (165).

It is highly significant that the original etymological meaning of the word *crisis* in Greek does not have the present negative connotation it presently has in English and in other modern languages.[1] It originally meant a propitious "opportunity" in the wake of a serious obstacle to pause and look back at the journey so far, in order to give it a radically new direction. In fact, only a crisis brings real change. In this vein, the *crisis* of our common home, with all its grim prospects, holds a beacon of hope for humanity to enter into a new *kairos*. The crisis may offer at the same time a historical opportunity to rebuild our common planetary home and heal the ruptured bonds of fellowship among the whole of humanity and with the rest of the biotic community. As Professor Myles Allen of Oxford University writes in the foreword to the present volume, Pope Francis in *Laudato Si'* provides us with the inspiration and moral compass to embark on this journey together.

Responding to the crisis of our common home can indeed be a truly "ecumenical" experience that can re-create "one home" (*oikos* + *monos*) for the whole of humanity. What is

---

1. See Joshtrom Isaac Kureethadam, *Creation in Crisis: Science, Ethics, Theology* (New York: Orbis, 2014), 373.

important is that we act together, now, as the question is extremely urgent. Faced with the crisis of our common home, it is time to make "a new beginning." Pope Francis echoes the courageous challenge that was presented by the *Earth Charter* at the beginning of the new millennium:

> As never before in history, common destiny beckons us to seek a new beginning . . . Let ours be a time remembered for the awakening of a new reverence for life, the firm resolve to achieve sustainability, the quickening of the struggle for justice and peace, and the joyful celebration of life.[2] (207)

Laudato Si' for all the serious warnings which the pope makes and endorses about the alarming state of our common home "is a work imbued with Christian hope," as Ashley Beck has noted.[3] According to Pope Francis, "Humanity still has the ability to work together in building our common home" (13); "Men and women are still capable of intervening positively" (58); and "All is not lost. Human beings, while capable of the worst, are also capable of rising above themselves, choosing again what is good, and making a new start" (205).

The true foundation of our hope rests on our faith that we are assisted in the task of rebuilding our common home by the love and strength of the Lord.

> God, who calls us to generous commitment and to give him our all, offers us the light and the strength needed to continue on our way. In the heart of this world, the Lord of life, who loves us so much, is always present. He does not abandon us, he does not leave us alone, for he has

2. *Earth Charter*, The Hague (29 June 2000).

3. See Ashley Beck, "Prophecy and Hope: An Initial Appraisal of *Laudato Si'*," *The Pastoral Review* 11/5 (2015), 7.

united himself definitively to our earth, and his love constantly impels us to find new ways forward. *Praise be to
him*! (245)

It is significant that the encyclical *Laudato Si'* was issued
on the day of the solemnity of Pentecost in 2015, a day in
which Christians all over the world commemorate the work
of the Spirit of God in creation and in redemption. As generations of believers have prayed down the centuries, we too
can pray today: "Send forth your Spirit, O Lord, and renew
the face of the earth" (see Ps 104:30). We pray that the same
Spirit who hovered over the primordial waters at the dawn
of creation, the same Spirit who hovered over Mary at the
incarnation, the same Spirit who raised Jesus from the claws
of death, may also inflame many hearts with the zeal for the
care of our common planetary home. We can thus become,
as Pope Francis invited humanity in his very first *Urbi et Orbi*
Message on Easter Sunday 2013, "channels through which
God can water the earth, protect all creation and make justice
and peace flourish." We conclude with the very prayer that
closes the encyclical letter of Pope Francis:

Father, we praise you with all your creatures.
They came forth from your all-powerful hand;
     they are yours, filled with your presence and your tender love.
Praise be to you!

Son of God, Jesus,
     through you all things were made.
You were formed in the womb of Mary our Mother,
     you became part of this earth,
and you gazed upon this world with human eyes.
Today you are alive in every creature
     in your risen glory.
Praise be to you!

Holy Spirit, by your light
you guide this world towards the Father's love
and accompany creation as it groans in travail.
You also dwell in our hearts
and you inspire us to do what is good.
Praise be to you!

Triune Lord,
wondrous community of infinite love,
teach us to contemplate you
in the beauty of the universe,
for all things speak of you.
Awaken our praise and thankfulness
for every being that you have made.
Give us the grace to feel profoundly joined
to everything that is.

God of love, show us our place in this world
as channels of your love
for all the creatures of this earth,
for not one of them is forgotten in your sight.
Enlighten those who possess power and money
that they may avoid the sin of indifference,
that they may love the common good,
advance the weak,
and care for this world in which we live.
The poor and the earth are crying out.
O Lord, seize us with your power and light,
help us to protect all life,
to prepare for a better future,
for the coming of your Kingdom
of justice, peace, love and beauty.
Praise be to you!
Amen.